TROLL
FAMOUS PEOPLE

TROLL
FAMOUS PEOPLE

by
Kenneth and Valerie McLeish
Illustrated by Damon Burnard,
and Andrew Snell

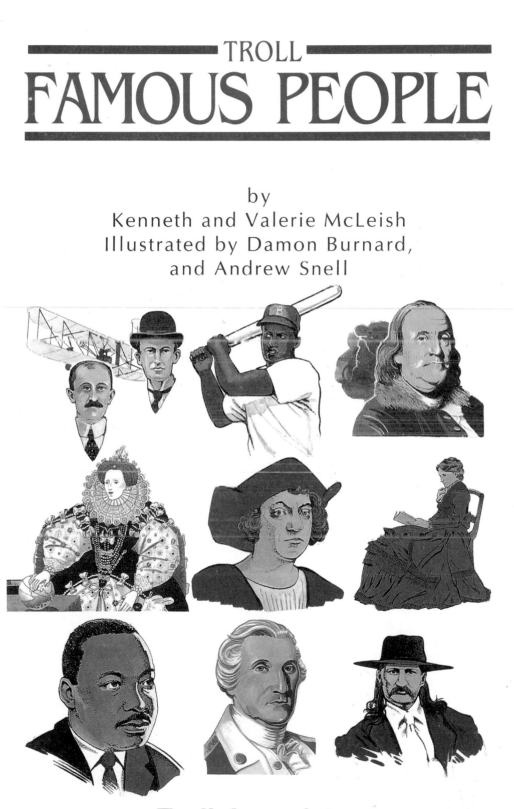

Troll Associates

Library of Congress Cataloging-in-Publication Data

McLeish, Kenneth.
    Famous people / by Kenneth and Valerie McLeish; illustrated by
Damon Burnard...[et al.].
        p.   cm.
    Summary: Profiles historical and contemporary world leaders,
athletes, artists, musicians, explorers, scientists, and other
famous people.
    ISBN 0-8167-2238-2 (lib. bdg.)   ISBN 0-8167-2239-0 (pbk.)
    1. Biography—Juvenile literature.   [1. Biography.]   I. McLeish,
Valerie, 1940-   .   II. Burnard, Damon, ill.   III. Title.
CT104.M44   1991
920—dc20
[B]   90-37910

Published in the U.S.A. by Troll Associates, Inc.,
Produced for Troll Associates, Inc., by
Joshua Morris Publishing Inc. in association
with Harper Collins.
Copyright © 1991 by Harper Collins.
Copyright © 1991 Kenneth and Valerie McLeish.
Based on the Collins Illustrated Encyclopedia
of Famous People.
All rights reserved.
Printed in Belgium.
10 9 8 7 6 5 4 3 2 1

CONTENTS

THE ARTS . . . 7

LEADERS . . . 25

PEOPLE OF ACTION . . . 44

SCIENTISTS . . . 60

SPORT AND ENTERTAINMENT . . . 72

THINKERS AND INVENTORS . . .85

INDEX . . . 95

THE ARTS

AESOP
6th century BC?
Greek storyteller

Aesop is an almost legendary person. The ancient Greek historian Herodotus said in his *Histories* that Aesop was a slave living on the island of Samos. Aesop became popular for his stories, with which he entertained the royal courts.

The kind of story Aesop told, and was said to have invented, was the "fable." This is a short tale or joke ending with a moral lesson. Many of these are familiar to us, such as "a wolf in sheep's clothing." Aesop's tales were always about animals, to which he gave human characteristics and failings in order to mock human behavior. Many of Aesop's fables are still told today. The most famous are "The Tortoise and the Hare" and "The Fox and the Grapes."

ALCOTT, Louisa May
1832–88
U.S. author

Louisa May Alcott was born in Germantown, Pennsylvania, but was raised in Boston and Concord, Massachusetts. Her father was Bronson Alcott, a famous educator and lecturer. The Alcott family did not have much money. So Louisa began at an early age to help support the family as a household servant, teacher, and seamstress (someone who sews for money).

At 16, Alcott began writing stories that she hoped would be published. Her most successful book for children was *Little Women*, which told about life in a family much like her own. It was published in two parts in 1868 and 1869. She continued the story of this family in *Little Men* (1871) and *Jo's Boys* (1886).

Alcott wrote more than 200 books and stories for children and adults. Her other books for young readers include *An Old-Fashioned Girl* (1870), *Eight Cousins* (1874), *Rose in Bloom* (1876), and *Under the Lilacs* (1879).

ANDERSEN, Hans Christian
1805–75
Danish writer

Andersen is best known for his fairy tales for children. He took ideas from folk tales and wrote 168 stories. A favorite tale is "The Snow Queen," about a boy kidnapped by the wicked Snow Queen and saved only when kindness melts the ice-splinter she had lodged in his heart. Another is "The Ugly Duckling," about a little bird who hates himself because he is so ugly when compared with all the other ducklings. However, the little bird grows into a beautiful swan.

This scene shows the moment in Hans Christian Andersen's story when the Ugly Duckling, now grown up, realizes that he is a swan after all.

BACH, Johann Sebastian
1685–1750
German composer

Bach's first training was from his brother. He practiced the harpsichord, violin, and organ. When he was old enough, he became a choirboy and learned composing from the church organist. At the age of 18, he became an organist in the Lutheran church. He had to train the choir, write the music, play for all the services, provide music for town entertainments, and teach in the choirboys' school. Many other musicians of the day – for example, Vivaldi – became famous by performing all over Europe, but Bach remained a church musician, serving one community. At 38 he took the job of director of music at St. Thomas's School in Leipzig, and stayed there for the rest of his life.

Bach wrote both sacred (for church use) and secular (for concerts) music. For the church, he composed the music for hymns, anthems, and masses (including the *Mass in B minor* for soloists, choir, and orchestra). For the concert performer, he wrote sonatas, suites, and concertos (including the six *Brandenburg Concertos* for solo instruments and orchestra). He wrote over 500 works for the keyboard. They include the well-known *Toccata and Fugue in D minor* for organ and *The Well-Tempered Clavier*, for harpsichord.

BARRIE, Sir James Matthew
1860–1937
Scottish writer

J.M. Barrie wrote several novels and plays for adults. But his best-known work is the children's play, *Peter Pan* (1904). It is the story of a boy who can fly and lives in a land where he never has to grow up. Peter Pan takes three children – Wendy, John, and Michael – to visit his home in Neverland, where they have many adventures with the fairy Tinker Bell, the Indian princess Tiger Lily, and the evil pirate Captain Hook.

BAUM, L. (Lyman) Frank
1856–1919
U.S. author

Baum wrote one of the most popular children's books of all time, *The Wonderful Wizard of Oz* (1900). He was born in Chittenango, New York, and became a magazine editor. His first book, *Father Goose: His Story* (1899), was very successful. The next year, he finished his first Oz book.

Baum wrote a total of 14 books about the magical land of Oz, including *Ozma of Oz* (1907) and *The Scarecrow of Oz* (1915). He also wrote other books for children. Many of his books were adapted for production on the stage.

In 1939, the adventures of Dorothy, Toto, the Scarecrow, the Tin Man, and the Cowardly Lion in *The Wonderful Wizard of Oz* were made into a very successful movie, *The Wizard of Oz*.

James Barrie's magic character Peter Pan casts a watchful eye over wicked Captain Hook.

Frank Baum wrote fourteen books about the magical land of Oz. The first, *The Wonderful Wizard of Oz*, told the adventures of Dorothy, a little girl from Kansas, and her dog, Toto. The story was later made into the movie, *The Wizard of Oz*.

BEETHOVEN, Ludwig van
1770–1827
German composer

Until Beethoven was over 30, he was chiefly famous as a pianist. He was known especially for his improvisations (making up music on the spot). Sometimes he played whole long pieces of music. At other times his music reminded his audience of scenes or feelings: battles, a peaceful countryside, an angry person talking to a calm one, and so on. Afterward, he would often write these improvisations down (for example, the two piano sonatas later nicknamed "The Moonlight Sonata" and "The Pastoral Sonata"). He also composed symphonies, concertos, and string quartets. In his early works, Beethoven composed in the classical tradition of Mozart and Haydn, with whom Beethoven studied music in Vienna.

Beethoven began to lose his hearing when he was in his twenties. By the time he had reached his fifties, he had become completely deaf. However, he continued to compose until he died, aged 57.

As early as 1798, Beethoven's doctors told him that he was going deaf and that in a few years he would hear no outside sounds at all. Beethoven and his doctors tried various means to save his hearing, but all failed. By the time he was 50, he was entirely deaf. People had to write down any remarks they made to him, and he could hear none of his music being performed. When he played the piano himself, he pounded so hard that he broke the strings. When he was conducting, he had to be turned around to see the audience applauding.

Like all musicians, Beethoven was able to "hear" music in his mind, and so he could continue composing. He came to be considered one of the greatest artistic geniuses in history. His nine symphonies, five piano concertos, 16 string quartets, and over 30 piano sonatas are among the most often performed and best loved of all classical music.

BRAHMS, Johannes
1833–97
German composer

Brahms is known for his tuneful, romantic music. Although his parents were poor, they managed to pay for their musically talented son to have piano lessons in Hamburg, where the boy grew up. By the time Brahms was 19, his playing and composing had impressed the most important musicians of the day.

Brahms spent nine months of each year at home in Vienna, composing, conducting, or playing at concerts. Two or three times a year, he went on concert tours. And every summer he went to the Austrian Alps, Switzerland, or Italy, often working on new pieces while he was away. He composed four symphonies, four concertos, and other large scale works. *A German Requiem*, for example, was written between 1857 and 1868 for soloists, chorus, and orchestra. But his favorite music was on a smaller scale. Brahms wrote dozens of songs, piano pieces, short orchestral pieces, and chamber music which he and his friends often played themselves. He also composed *Wiegenlied*, which means "Lullaby." It is one of the best-loved and familiar lullabies in the world.

BURNETT, Frances Hodgson
1849–1924
English-born U.S. author

Born in Manchester, England, Burnett moved to Knoxville, Tennessee, when she was 16 years old. While still a teenager, she wrote stories for U.S. magazines. Her first novel, *That Lass O' Lowrie's* (1877), was set in England.

Burnett wrote other novels but she is most famous for her books for young people. These include *Little Lord Fauntleroy* (1886), *A Little Princess* (1905), and *The Secret Garden* (1911). *Little Lord Fauntleroy* became very popular and set a style for boy's clothing.

CARROLL, Lewis
1832–98
English author

Born in Daresbury, England, Lewis Carroll was the pen name of Charles Lutwidge Dodgson. He was a professor of mathematics at Oxford University in England. A shy person with adults, he enjoyed being with children. He first wrote the story *Alice's Adventures in Wonderland* (1865) as a present for a little girl named Alice Liddell. Carroll continued Alice's adventures in *Through the Looking Glass and What Alice Found There* (1871).

Carroll also wrote other children's books as well as books for adults about mathematics. But the "Alice" books went on to become two of the most famous books in English literature. Filled with funny and imaginative characters such as the Mad Hatter, the March Hare, the Cheshire Cat, and the White Rabbit, these books have long been enjoyed by both children and adults.

The characters created in the stories by Lewis Carroll have captured the imagination of children for over 100 years.

CASSATT, Mary
1844–1926
U.S. painter

Born in Pittsburgh, Pennsylvania, Mary Cassatt spent most of her life in France. She began showing her paintings in Paris in the early 1870s. In France, she became friends with some of the great French artists of the time. Many of them painted in a style called impressionism. Their use of strong, bright colors influenced Cassatt's own style.

Cassatt is most famous for her paintings of everyday life, especially of loving moments between mothers and young children. After 1900, her eyesight started to fail, and she stopped painting by 1914.

Stories that travelers supposedly told one another on the long ride from London to Canterbury are known as *The Canterbury Tales.* In fact, they were really tales written by Geoffrey Chaucer. Among the most famous of *The Canterbury Tales* are "The Knight's Tale," "The Nun's Tale," and "The Wife of Bath's Tale."

CHAUCER, Geoffrey
1340?–1400
English poet

Chaucer was first a soldier, then an ambassador to several European countries. He was fascinated by the folk tales and poetry of the countries he visited, and he set out to produce original English works of the same kind. Among his best-known poems are *Troilus and Criseyde*, a love story set during the Trojan War, and *The Canterbury Tales*.

The people in *The Canterbury Tales* are pilgrims, riding from London to St. Thomas à Becket's shrine at Canterbury, England. To pass time on the journey, each of them tells a story. Some of the stories are funny, others serious. Chaucer's stories are written in rhyming verse and are full of humor and insight into medieval life.

CHOPIN, Frédéric
1810–49
Polish-born French musician

Born in Warsaw, Poland, Chopin trained as a pianist and composer. At the age of 19, he began giving concerts throughout Europe. He settled in Paris, giving concerts, teaching piano, and composing. Much of his music is filled with sounds based on Polish folk songs and dances.

Chopin wrote two piano concertos and three sonatas. Apart from these, most of his works are short compositions: nocturnes, études ("studies"), waltzes, preludes, mazurkas, and polonaises. He died of tuberculosis at age 39.

DA VINCI, Leonardo
1452–1519
Italian artist and scientist

Leonardo was one of the most gifted figures of the period known as the Italian Renaissance, when Europeans were rediscovering the arts and sciences of ancient Greece and Rome. He was not only a great painter and illustrator, but also a brilliant sculptor, architect, and engineer.

Leonardo worked as an artist for the dukes of Florence and Milan. Many of his paintings were on religious themes. In them Leonardo interpreted the Bible in an entirely original and moving way. In *The Last Supper*, for example, he painted Jesus and the disciples at a long table facing the viewer so that we seem to be on the other side of the table, sharing the meal.

Leonardo's style was highly realistic. He had a genius for capturing the outlines of moving bodies, from a rearing horse to a bustling crowd. His portraits show character as well as appearance. Who can tell, for example, what the *Mona Lisa* is thinking? From her clothes and surroundings, we can see what sort of person she is. But we also get the feeling that she is thinking about something. Leonardo could capture people's thoughts on his canvas through their expressions and in this way give his pictures life.

Leonardo's reputation as one of the greatest artists in world history, however, comes also from many other skills. He was interested in music and theater. He wrote poetry. Above all, he studied science and technology. He filled notebook after notebook with sketches and descriptions of rocks, plants, and the flow of water. He also looked closely at people and animals to understand how animals move and the way faces and bodies change as people age. He studied the science of movement and drew plans for all kinds of mechanical marvels, including a submarine, a fixed-wing aircraft, a tank, and a helicopter.

Leonardo had a special combination of vast scientific knowledge and an inventive imagination. However, his brilliant thinking was ahead of his time, which explains why some of his inventions were not realistic. But the range and quality of his work make him one of the greatest geniuses the world has ever known.

This famous painting the *Mona Lisa* by Leonardo da Vinci contains a mystery. What is she thinking, and why is she smiling?

DEFOE, Daniel
1660–1731
English writer

Defoe wrote hundreds of newspaper articles and books on all kinds of subjects. Born in London, he spent most of his working life as a political journalist. Later in his life, he turned to writing novels, including his famous *Robinson Crusoe*. Written in 1719, it told the story of a shipwrecked sailor who survives on a desert island. In the end, Crusoe is rescued with his servant Friday, whom he had earlier saved from cannibals. He then takes Friday home to England to show him what "civilized" life is like. Another famous novel Daniel Defoe wrote was *Moll Flanders* (1722).

Daniel Defoe's most famous novel *Robinson Crusoe* is a tale of how two men survived on a desert island for many years. Here, Crusoe dreams of his long-lost home.

DEGAS, Hilaire Germain Edgar
1834–1917
French painter

Degas, born in Paris, was the son of a banker. Having a keen interest in art, Degas studied Japanese prints and experimented with the new hobby of photography. In the 1870s, he began painting subjects from modern life. Unlike the works of most artists of his time, his paintings were similar to the scenes people like to see in photographs.

Degas was one of a group of young painters who became known as "Impressionists." Like them, he was fascinated by the effect that movement has on light and color. He painted racetrack scenes, concentrating on the crowds as well as the blurred shapes of horses and jockeys rushing past. He painted acrobats and circus performers working, dressing, and bathing. Later, he turned to the theater. His paintings and pastel sketches showed actors, singers, comedians, and the orchestra. Perhaps his best-known subjects for painting were ballet dancers exercising and performing.

When Degas was 60, he began to go blind and found sculpture easier than painting. One of his first sculptures caused a scandal. It showed a young ballet dancer, modeled in wax, wearing a real ballet dress, complete with tutu (stiff skirt) and shoes. At the time, people thought his mixture of "art" and "reality" shocking. Many called Degas a fraud. Today, this statue, along with other sculptures and pastels of ballet dancers, are among the most popular works by Degas.

DICKENS, Charles
1812–70
English writer

Dickens began his writing career as a law reporter for a London paper. In the 1830s he began writing articles about ordinary people and places. These appeared in an evening paper and were later published as *Sketches by Boz*. Dickens was encouraged by their success to begin his first novel, in 1836. It is about a group of friends led by a fat, cheerful character called Mr. Pickwick. Like most of Dickens's work it was first published in parts. When it was published as a single book, entitled *The Pickwick Papers*, it became so popular that Dickens was able to give up journalism and become a full-time novelist.

Dickens wrote a bestseller each year for several years. His novels described the way people lived in England during his time. He wrote about all kinds of people and their daily lives, often inventing extraordinary characters, based on people he had encountered as a reporter. With stories such as *Oliver Twist* and *Nicholas Nickleby*, Dickens gave vivid pictures of the best and worst sides of the life of his time. Many people were made to realize for the first time that such poverty, cruelty, and suffering existed in nineteenth century Britain.

As Dickens's fame grew, he began to make tours. He traveled all over Britain and the United States reading to audiences to raise money for charity. He would plan new novels while he traveled and write them down when touring stopped each summer. Some of his finest books were written in this way, including *David Copperfield*, the novel he thought was his masterpiece. He based the story on his own life. It tells of an unhappy badly treated boy who grew up to become a successful writer.

Charles Dickens at his desk. Several of his novels have been made into successful movies, including *Great Expectations* and *Oliver Twist*. That novel was also turned into the Broadway hit and Oscar-winning musical, *Oliver*.

DOYLE, Arthur Conan
1859–1930
British writer

Doyle invented the famous detective character Sherlock Holmes, who solved crimes with his amazing intelligence and powers of observation. Holmes appeared in dozens of short stories and longer works, such as *A Study in Scarlet* (the first Holmes novel) and *The Hound of the Baskervilles*.

Doyle was born in Edinburgh, Scotland. He studied medicine and became a doctor. When Doyle began writing, he modeled his character Holmes on one of his former medical professors. Holmes's character is so convincing that many people believe he is a real person. Letters are still being sent to him at his fictitious address: 221B Baker Street, London.

Doyle also wrote several other kinds of books. *The Lost World* is about explorers who find living dinosaurs and Stone Age people in the jungles of South America. *The White Company* is about a group of knights in the Middle Ages.

GAUGUIN, Paul
1848-1903
French painter

Born in Paris, Gauguin was a cadet in the merchant marine when he was 17. He returned to France and worked as a banker until, at the age of 35, he decided to devote his life to art. He cut himself off from everything that reminded him of his earlier life, including his wife and five children. He gave up everything that was not essential and lived in poverty.

Gaugin's paintings outraged art critics because they showed things not as they were but as his imagination saw them. He liked to combine colors on the canvas to create unusual, dreamlike effects. He felt, for example, that if the artist "saw" a yellow sea or red grass, that was how it should be painted.

In 1891, Gauguin made another unexpected move in search of the paradise of his dreams. He went to Tahiti in the South Seas, where the air was clear, the colors were bright, and where he imagined life was simple and childlike. He painted people going about their ordinary lives – working, playing, and bathing. These are the paintings for which he is still best known.

Gauguin moved to the Marquesas Islands in 1901, where he died two years later.

GRAHAME, Kenneth
1859–1932
Scottish author

Born in Edinburgh, Scotland, Grahame studied at Oxford University in England and worked for the Bank of England. His writings are noted for their humor and charm. Grahame is best known for writing the children's classic *The Wind in the Willows* (1908). It is about the adventures of Toad, Rat, Mole, Badger, and other small animals. The tale began as a series of letters to Grahame's son Alastair, who was known as "Mouse." It was made into a play called *Toad of Toad Hall* in 1929.

Grahame's other books include *The Golden Age* (1895) and *Dream Days* (1898). The latter describes scenes of Grahame's childhood in England and includes the tale of "The Reluctant Dragon." Grahame also compiled the *Cambridge Book of Poetry for Young People* (1916).

GRIMM, Jakob Ludwig
1785–1863
German writer
  and

GRIMM, Wilhelm Karl
1786–1859
German writer

Born in Hanau, Germany, the Grimm brothers were scholars. They studied law and taught at the University of Berlin. The two brothers wrote many reference books, including the *German Dictionary*. Jakob Grimm also wrote the *German Grammar*. But the Grimms are most famous for their collection of folk tales and legends now known as *Grimm's Fairy Tales*.

Jakob and Wilhelm visited German villages and farms, asking people to tell stories they remembered hearing as children. The brothers then wrote them down. The *Fairy Tales* contain some of the best-loved children's stories ever published, including "Hansel and Gretel," "Rapunzel," "The Frog Prince," "Snow White and the Seven Dwarfs," and "Rumpelstiltskin."

The Grimms published their fairy tales in several volumes. By the time they finished their work, they had collected and retold 210 tales. Since then, their stories have been translated into about seventy different languages and are read throughout the world. The first English version was published in 1823.

In this famous scene from Kenneth Grahame's *The Wind in the Willows*, Toad makes a daring escape dressed as a washerwoman.

HOMER (Homeros)
8th century BC
Greek poet

Homer was famous as a poet and storyteller. Almost nothing is known of his life. Some scholars do not believe that he was a real person. According to tradition, Homer was blind and told his long stories (called *epics*) aloud from memory. The first

Homer's epic poem of the siege of the city of Troy was first told in ancient Greece, and to this day it has provided thrilling material for motion pictures and adventure films.

IRVING, Washington
1783–1859
U.S. author and diplomat

Irving's humorous stories and essays poked fun at New York's fashionable people. He was the first American writer to gain fame in Europe as well as the United States.

Born in New York City, Irving was not very interested in school, although he did study to become a lawyer.

Irving first became known as a writer in 1809. Under the name of Diedrich Knickerbocker, he published *A History of New York From the Beginning of the World to the End of the Dutch Dynasty.* It was full of comic tales about New York when it was ruled by the Dutch.

Irving's most famous works made the short story popular. In "Rip Van Winkle," Rip falls asleep for 20 years and awakens to find everything different. In "The Legend of Sleepy Hollow," schoolmaster Ichabod Crane meets a headless horseman.

Washington Irving soon became America's most popular writer. He spent much of his time traveling in Europe. He also served as a diplomat in Spain, but he was always gathering material for his books. Returning to his home, "Sunnyside," in Tarrytown, New York, Irving turned to history and biography. His visits to the American West resulted in two books. And just before his death, Irving completed a five-volume biography of George Washington.

set, called the *Iliad,* takes place during the final year of the Trojan War, when the Greeks attacked Troy in Anatolia (Turkey) to win back Helen, their stolen queen. The trick they used to get inside the city (hiding inside a huge wooden horse) is one of the most famous of all ancient myths. The main theme of the *Iliad* is the quarrel between the Greek hero Achilles and the Trojan hero Hector. Achilles killed Hector outside the walls of Troy.

The second set of stories, the *Odyssey,* takes place after the defeat of Troy. It tells of the 10-year-long adventures of the Greek hero Odysseus (Ulysses) as he journeys home to Greece. On the way, he faces such monsters as the one-eyed, flesh-eating Cyclops and an enchantress named Circe. The tale ends with Odysseus (thought to be long dead by his family) entering his own palace in disguise. He saves his wife Penelope from men who have been trying to marry her against her will.

Washington Irving wrote the famous tale of Rip Van Winkle, who slept for twenty years.

An Indian elephant, one of the animals that English writer Rudyard Kipling encountered while he was living in India, where he was born. Later, he included elephants in many of his stories, including, of course, Kala Nag in *The Jungle Book*. It was published in 1894 when Kipling and his American wife were living in Brattleboro, Vermont.

KIPLING, Rudyard
1865–1936
English writer

Kipling was born in Bombay, India, but went to school in England. He wrote about Indian life and customs in his short stories and poems. He won the Nobel Prize for literature in 1907, becoming the first English writer so honored.

He returned to India in 1882 to work on a newspaper. He soon began to write poems and short stories. *Barrack-Room Ballads* is a collection of poems about the British Empire. His novel, *Kim*, tells about an Irish boy whose parents died in India.

Kipling also wrote many books for children: *The Jungle Book, Just So Stories, Puck of Pook's Hill,* and *Stalky and Co.* He is also known for his poems "Gunga Din" and "If."

LONDON, Jack
1876–1916
U.S. writer

Born in San Francisco, Jack London was an author who wrote about survival. As a teenager, he worked as a docker, seal hunter, and pirate. He also took part in the Klondike Gold Rush of 1897. At 19, he began to write stories for newspapers, usually about the gold prospectors, fur trappers, sailors, and fishermen he had met on his travels. Soon he was one of America's best-known authors.

London's stories are collected in many books. But he is also famous for his novels. Of those, *The*

Call of the Wild (1903) is probably his best known. It is about a dog named Buck, who is taken from sunny California to work as a sled dog in the bitterly cold Yukon territory. Two other London novels are considered classics: *The Sea-Wolf* (1904), about a pirate and the city couple he kidnaps, and *White Fang* (1906), about the taming of a wolf.

MELVILLE, Herman
1819–91
U.S. writer

After his father died, young Melville worked at several jobs to help support his family. He went to sea as a cabin boy in 1837. He wrote about this experience in *Redburn* (1849). When he worked aboard a whaling ship in 1841, he left the ship in the South Seas and lived on several islands with the natives over a period of two years. He related this experience in *Typee* (1846) and *Omoo* (1847). When he reached the island of Hawaii in 1843, he joined the U.S. Navy in order to get home. His novel, *White-Jacket* (1850) was about this experience.

In 1850, he moved from New York City to Pittsfield, Massachusetts, where he became friends with many other writers of the day. It was here, in 1851, that he wrote his most famous story, *Moby-Dick*. Moby Dick is a great white whale that is being hunted by Ahab, captain of the whaling ship

A scene from the story of Moby Dick, the great white whale.

Pequod. Ahab wants to kill the whale because Moby Dick had bitten off the captain's leg at an earlier time. When *Moby-Dick* was not well received by the reading public, Melville became depressed. It was not until after he died that the story became famous because of its many hidden meanings.

Melville finally decided that he could not make a living by just writing. He moved his family back to New York City and took a job as a customs inspector. After that, he wrote stories and poems for his own pleasure. In 1888, he began to write *Billy Budd*, but it was not published until 1924, long after his death.

MICHELANGELO
1475–1564
Italian artist

Michelangelo's family name was Buonarroti. When he was 12, he began to learn how to paint fresco, a process of painting with watercolors on wet plaster for walls and ceilings. The powerful Duke Lorenzo de' Medici of Florence, who took the boy into his service, thought highly of his talent. Michelangelo spent the next three years studying and copying the sculpture of ancient Rome. He was a very religious Christian, and from his teenage years onward he tried to blend Bible subjects with Greek ideas about making statues. His *David* is modeled on statues of Apollo, Hermes, and other Greek gods. It was the largest marble statue carved in Italy since the end of the Roman Empire.

Michelangelo also spent much time in Rome. In 1508, Pope Julius II asked him to paint scenes from the Bible on the ceiling of the Sistine Chapel in the Vatican, the headquarters of the Catholic Church. This was a difficult task. It is now thought Michelangelo had to lie on a high platform, painting above his head, to cover a ceiling twice as big as a tennis court. He painted many subjects from the Bible's Old Testament, including three of the most important stories: the Creation, Adam and Eve, and Noah and the flood. The work took three years and has always been judged to be a supreme masterpiece.

Besides being a painter and sculptor, Michelangelo was a great architect. Back in Florence he worked on several building projects for the Medici family. Then, when he was 59, he was recalled to Rome to paint the most awesome Bible scene of all: *The Last Judgment.* He began the work in 1534 and finished it seven years later.

Michelangelo spent the last years of his life in Rome. At the age of 71 he redesigned St. Peter's, the huge church that is the center of Roman Catholic worship in the world. He also made drawings of the Crucifixion of St. Peter. At this time he wrote some of his best poetry and spent much time praying and reading the Bible. When he died at 89, Michelangelo was thought of as the greatest artist of all time – an opinion that is still widely held today.

MOSES, Grandma (Anna Mary)
1860–1961
U.S. painter

Grandma Moses started painting when she was 76 years old. She stayed active almost until her death. Her colorful and lively works are simple but realistic scenes of farm life, called American primitives.

Born Anna Mary Robertson in Greenwich, New York, she was married to Thomas Moses in 1887. She lived the hard life of a farm wife. Throughout much of her life, she stitched pictures on canvas. Only after arthritis made it hard for her to hold a sewing needle did she start to paint.

Her paintings are based on memories of her youth in the late 1800s in Virginia and northern New York. She painted *The Old Oaken Bucket, Sugaring-Off, Out for the Christmas Trees,* and *Thanksgiving Turkey,* among others.

Her first exhibition was at the Museum of Modern Art in New York City in 1939. The art of Grandma Moses has become very popular through prints and Christmas cards.

After a life of farming, Grandma Moses began a career as an artist at the age of 76. Her paintings became very popular.

By the time Mozart was six years old, he was touring in concerts throughout Europe with his father and older sister, Maria Anna. He played the harpsichord, Maria Anna sang, and his father, Leopold Mozart, played the violin.

MOZART, Wolfgang Amadeus
1756–91
Austrian composer

When he was four years old, Mozart could play the harpsichord, a keyboard instrument like the piano. Before he was five he began making up music. By the time he was six he was giving concerts all over Europe. During his travels the young Mozart heard every kind of music being written and played in Europe at the time. He grew up playing or conducting at concerts and teaching the harpsichord and piano. He wrote and conducted operas and other musical works for anyone who would pay him, but it was difficult to make a living this way.

When Mozart was 31, his father died. Mozart had to depend more and more on the help and support of his wife Constanze, because they owed a lot of money. He was constantly overworked. As well as traveling to dozens of cities each year to play and conduct, Mozart was pouring out new works, sometimes at the rate of one a week. Working so hard was very bad for his health. In 1791, aged only 35, he died.

During his short life, which was exciting and busy, Mozart wrote over 150 orchestral works – symphonies, serenades, and concertos – as well as sonatas, string quartets, and other chamber music. He wrote 22 operas, including *The Marriage of Figaro, Don Giovanni,* and *The Magic Flute.* He also composed masses and other works for the church.

There are few people who cannot find at least one piece of Mozart's work enjoyable. For many music lovers he is the finest classical composer who ever lived.

O'KEEFFE, Georgia
1887–1986
U.S. painter

O'Keeffe's art is inspired by nature. Her best known subjects are flowers and bleached animal bones, rolling hills, clouds, and rocks of the desert, which she painted in a highly personal style.

Born in Sun Prairie, Wisconsin, O'Keeffe studied at the Art Institute of Chicago and the Art Students League in New York City. She worked

Georgia O'Keeffe found the inspiration for her paintings in her observations of nature.

briefly as a commercial artist, then gave up painting until she enrolled at Columbia University Teachers College. She then taught art in schools around the country.

Her art was first shown in 1916 at "291," an experimental art gallery in New York City. In 1924, O'Keeffe married Alfred Stieglitz, an American photographer who established "291." Starting in 1929, she spent more and more of her time in New Mexico, and she settled permanently near Taos in 1949.

The forms in Georgia O'Keeffe's paintings are smoothed, simplified, and painted with strong, clear colors. Most of her works reflect her affection for the desert landscape of the American Southwest.

PERRAULT, Charles
1628–1703
French writer

Charles Perrault was born in Paris. He was the younger brother of the famous scientist and architect Claude Perrault. Although Charles Perrault was well known in his time as a poet and critic, he is best remembered today for his book of folk and fairy tales. The book, *Tales of Mother Goose* (1697),

Mother Goose's stories, such as "Tom Thumb" and "Puss in Boots," have enchanted millions of children who probably never knew that the "mother" was really a Frenchman, Charles Perrault.

contained eight stories that Perrault had collected. Most of them are very familiar, such as "Puss in Boots," "Bluebeard," and "Tom Thumb."

Perrault also helped to start "the quarrel between the ancients and the moderns." This was an argument between writers who thought that the culture of ancient Greece and Rome was the best that had ever been and writers who believed that their own seventeenth-century culture was superior. Perrault was one of the leaders of the group that favored "modern" literature, philosophy, and science.

PICASSO, Pablo Ruiz y
1881–1973
Spanish artist

Picasso showed his talent as a child. His father was a drawing teacher. Pablo learned to paint by imitating such great artists of the past as Rembrandt and Goya. At the age of 14 his pictures were good enough to show in art exhibitions and to sell.

When Picasso was 23, he moved to Paris. He admired the lively music-hall posters and paintings of the French artist Henri de Toulouse-Lautrec. Picasso began to make his own pictures of comedians, singers, and acrobats. But he showed the figures resting, or standing in silent solemn groups. The background color of many of these paintings was blue. This, added to the sadness in many of them, has led people to call this his "blue period."

Several years later, Picasso saw an exhibition of tribal masks from Africa. He liked them and began to use rectangular, shield-, or diamond-shaped faces like those carved in wood and decorated with streaks of paint and zigzags in his paintings. With a friend, the painter Georges Braque, he invented a new way of painting. The idea was to find basic signs for suggesting objects and the contrasts of light and shade, as in the work of Paul Cézanne. They divided the figure into basic forms – cylinders, triangles, rectangles, and above all, cubes. The new style was called Cubism. The way Picasso used cubism was probably the most important work of any artist of the twentieth century. Picasso went on using it himself for over 10 years and produced some of his best paintings in the style. At the same time he and Braque were experimenting with other new processes. They invented collage, which was making pictures by sticking scraps of paper onto the canvas. Another creation was assemblage, which was making sculptures by joining together scraps of material, such as wood, metal, and cloth.

In the 1920s, Picasso began drawing and painting in classical style, borrowing ideas from ancient Greece and Rome. Then, in the next decade, he was influenced by the Surrealists. They were a group of painters who painted fantastic images, mixing dream and reality. Picasso made violent scenes of bullfights, illustrations for Cervantes's novel *Don Quixote*, and dozens of drawings of artists (including himself) and their models. One of Picasso's most famous paintings was *Guernica*.

Of all the modern artists Picasso had the widest range of talents. As well as paintings and drawings, he made sculptures, ceramics (decorated pottery), prints, and cloth designs. Many people regard him as the greatest twentieth century artist, the modern equivalent of Goya, Rembrandt, and the other geniuses he had copied as a boy.

Potter illustrated her books featured scenes from the countryside in northern England, where she made her home.

Beatrix Potter painted the lifelike pictures that appear in her stories of Peter Rabbit, Tom Kitten and Jemima Puddle-Duck.

POE, Edgar Allan
1809–49
U.S. poet and writer

Poe was admired as a poet as well as a writer. He successfully published a collection of poems, *The Raven and Other Poems*. But he is best known for his mysteries. These include horror stories and some of the first detective stories ever written.

Poe liked to set his stories in dark, lonely houses at night or during storms. Many of his stories have been turned into films such as *The Pit and the Pendulum*.

POTTER, Helen Beatrix
1866–1943
English writer and illustrator

When Beatrix Potter was a child in London, she amused herself by drawing lifelike pictures of animals and plants. In the 1890s, she wrote and illustrated stories about small animals to send to a friend's sick child. She began publishing her stories in 1902 with *The Tale of Peter Rabbit*, her best-known and most-loved book. It was followed a year later by *The Tailor of Gloucester*.

During her life, Potter published more than 25 books about such characters as Jemima Puddle-Duck, Squirrel Nutkin, Tom Kitten, and Benjamin Bunny. The adventures of her animal characters were told in simple prose and were happy tales, often funny. The watercolor pictures with which

REMBRANDT (Rembrandt Harmenszoon van Rijn)
1606–69
Dutch painter

Rembrandt worked first in his native town, Leiden, as an art teacher and portrait painter, and then moved to Amsterdam. By the time he was 30 he was one of the most respected and popular painters in Holland. Rich people flocked to have their portraits painted, wearing their most gorgeous clothes, jewels, gold ornaments, and medals. Rembrandt painted their portraits, but he also had a sense of humor about them. Their clothes might be dazzling, but they themselves were not. He put in every wrinkle, gray hair, skin blemish, or frown. He also liked to paint groups.

People kept going back to Rembrandt, despite his boldness, because his work was magnificent. Rembrandt's mastery of *chiaroscuro* (strongly contrasting light and shade) was second to none. He imagined each painting as if it were lit by a single source of light, like a hidden spotlight, and then painted every tiny difference in light and shade.

In the 1650s, Rembrandt began to become less popular. Sitters complained that he was more interested in the details of his pictures than in painting people so that their friends could recognize them. Rembrandt turned to painting and drawing religious themes and produced one of his best-known works, *Saul and David*, a scene from the Bible. He also made many portraits of himself and his young son Titus and fine landscape drawings and etchings.

For 150 years after his death, although Rembrandt's use of light and dark was always considered superb, his reputation as an artist was not as high as he deserved. But in the nineteenth century, Rembrandt was considered to be one of the greatest of all painters. Years after his death, people began searching for his work and they discovered more than 300 etchings, 1,400 drawings, and 600 paintings. It is likely that many of these were fakes, or copies, done by assistants in his studio. Nonetheless, during his lifetime Rembrandt had produced a treasure house of art.

A self-portrait by Rembrandt, painted when he was an old man.

SENDAK, Maurice
1928–
U.S. writer and illustrator

Maurice Sendak was born in Brooklyn, New York. He was often sick as a child and spent much time at home, drawing pictures of what he saw from his window. He and his brother, Jack, would write stories and illustrate them with drawings. Maurice also loved comic books and movies, especially Mickey Mouse cartoons.

After he was graduated from high school, Sendak worked at F.A.O. Schwartz, a famous toy store in New York City. A visiting book editor saw Sendak's drawings and hired him to illustrate *Wonderful Farm* (1951), a children's book by Marcel Aymé. The following year he did the drawings for *A Hole Is To Dig*.

Kenny's Window (1956) was the first book that Maurice Sendak both wrote and illustrated. In 1964, he won the Caldecott Medal of the American Library Association for his illustrations in *Where the Wild Things Are* (1963). By 1985, this book had sold two and a half million copies. Other Sendak

Maurice Sendak wrote and illustrated some of his own stories.

books include *In the Night Kitchen* (1970); *Outside Over There* (1981), for which he received the American Book Award in 1982; and *Dear Milli* (1988).

SEWELL, Anna
1820–78
English writer

Born in Yarmouth, England, into a strict Quaker family, Anna Sewell sprained her ankle in a childhood accident. In spite of years of treatment, she improved only temporarily and was crippled for most of her life.

Her book, *Black Beauty*, the "autobiography of a horse," was written as a protest against cruelty to horses. It was published in 1877 and quickly became a classic, translated into many languages. Anna Sewell died the year after her book was published.

Anna Sewell's story of Black Beauty is one of the most famous stories ever written about a horse.

SHAKESPEARE, William
1564–1616
English playwright and poet

Shakespeare's father, a glovemaker, wanted his son to work in the family business. Many details of Shakespeare's life are a mystery so it is not certain that he did. It does seem that for a time he lived quietly in his hometown, Stratford-upon-Avon. He married Anne Hathaway, and they had several children. But when he was in his mid-20s, things changed. The theater was a popular entertainment at the time, and Shakespeare went to London to seek his fortune as an actor. He joined an acting company called the Lord Chamberlain's Men that was favored by the court of Queen Elizabeth the First.

As well as performing in plays, Shakespeare was writing them. His work was hugely successful. For the next 25 years, Shakespeare stayed in London, only going home to Stratford at holidays when the theaters were closed and when the royal court was out of town. He wrote over 30 plays (probably with the help of others) and several books of poetry. Then he went back to Stratford as unexpectedly as he had left it. He died there three years later at the age of 52.

Shakespeare wrote three main kinds of plays. Some were comedies, invented stories full of disguises, tricks, and songs. Others were histories, based on real-life characters (such as Julius Caesar and England's Henry the Eighth) and actual historical events. Later he wrote tragedies, serious plays dealing with such matters as nobility, trust, honor, and duty. Most of the plays are in verse. Some of them are magnificent poems written for the stage. These include *Romeo and Juliet* and *Antony and Cleopatra*, which are about doomed lovers, and *Othello* and *King Lear*, which are about powerful men destroyed by failings in their own character. His plays have been translated into almost every language and performed around the world from Shakespeare's time up until the present day.

Among Shakespeare's comedies, his best known are *A Midsummer Night's Dream, Twelfth Night*, and *As You Like It*. His most popular history plays include *Henry V, Richard III*, and *Henry IV Parts One and Two*. Of the tragedies (for which he is probably most famous of all), *Hamlet, Othello, Macbeth*, and *King Lear* are the best known. At the end of his life he wrote *The Tempest*, about a group of people shipwrecked on a magic island. Many people consider it his greatest play.

His best-known poems are a collection of over 100 sonnets (short rhyming verses), mostly on the theme of love.

Englishman William Shakespeare was not only a playwright, but an actor and a poet. He also helped direct the Globe Theatre in London where the theater company he belonged to, called *The King's Men*, was based. Shakespeare wrote more than 30 plays for the company to perform. His plays cover a wide range of subjects, including history, comedies, and tragedies.

STEINBECK, John
1902–68
U.S. novelist

Steinbeck wrote mainly about the lives of poor and unemployed people. His subjects were often unattractive or sad – despair, hunger, and the fury that comes from hopelessness. But he wrote about them in powerful language.

Steinbeck is one of the United States's most respected novelists. One of his best known books is *The Grapes of Wrath*, which won him the Pulitzer Prize for fiction in 1940. Another popular book written by Steinbeck is *Of Mice and Men*, which is about the friendship of two farm workers. In 1962, John Steinbeck won the Nobel Prize in literature.

STEVENSON, Robert Louis
1850–94
Scottish writer

Robert Louis Stevenson was born in Edinburgh, Scotland. He was sickly as a child and suffered from poor health all his life. In spite of this, he managed to travel all over the world and to become one of its most popular and successful writers.

Stevenson's first book was *An Inland Voyage* (1878), about a canoeing trip he took through France and Belgium. He later wrote several other travel books, plus essays and poems. The poems in his *A Child's Garden of Verses* (1885) are still read today. Stevenson is best known, however, for his novels. His first novel, *Treasure Island* (1883), is probably his best known. But *The Strange Case of Dr. Jekyll and Mr. Hyde* (1886), *Kidnapped* (1886), and *The Master of Ballantrae* (1889) remain popular as well.

Robert Louis Stevenson wrote some of the best-loved adventure stories in the English language.

SWIFT, Jonathan
1667–1745
English writer and minister

Jonathan Swift was a minister, but he is best known for his story of *Gulliver's Travels*, which he wrote in 1726. It is about Lemuel Gulliver, a doctor on a ship, who travels to different lands. Gulliver meets people who are smaller than he is (Lilliputians), people who are larger (Brobdingnagians), horses (Houyhnhnms), and savage animals (Yahoos). Swift had the different characters act just like some of the English people of his time. This is called satire, and Swift was called a satirist because of the way he wrote.

Swift was born in Ireland, but his parents were English. He went to England in about 1689 after he graduated from college. In 1695 he became a minister. Eventually, he became the head minister at St. Patrick's Cathedral in Dublin, Ireland. While there, he wrote such satires as *The Drapier's Letters* (1724) and *A Modest Proposal* (1729), both in favor of Irish independence from England.

In Swift's story *Gulliver's Travels*, Dr. Lemuel Gulliver is pinned down while he is asleep by tiny people called Lilliputians.

TCHAIKOVSKY, Peter Ilich
1840–93
Russian composer

Tchaikovsky was one of Russia's most famous composers of classical music. He wrote ballets and operas for the leading theaters in Russia and went on conducting tours in Russia, Germany, Italy, France, England, and the United States. But he seems to have preferred a quiet life at home, working at his music. He liked to compose in the morning, walk in the afternoon, then relax in the evening by playing cards or by writing letters.

Tchaikovsky loved reading, and he often wrote music based on the books he read. Two of his orchestral works, *Hamlet* and *Romeo and Juliet*, are based on plays by Shakespeare. His three ballets, *Swan Lake, The Nutcracker*, and *Sleeping Beauty*, are based on fairy tales. He also wrote the "1812" overture (a musical picture of a huge battle between the Russians and French at the time of Napoleon the First). Tchaikovsky's symphonies and concertos are among the most famous pieces of classical music ever composed.

TOLKIEN, J.R.R. (John Ronald Reuel)
1892–1973
English writer

Tolkien felt that if a fairy tale was worth reading, adults as well as children would enjoy it. He was an English professor, and his interest in the history of language and mythology is reflected in his stories. *The Hobbit*, a fantasy, was published in 1937. It is about the adventures of Bilbo Baggins, a creature called a hobbit, whose friends are dwarves and a wizard called Gandalf. They rob a dragon of its treasures and find a magic ring.

The same characters are also in *The Lord of the Rings*, a much longer, more complex story. Tolkien not only told an exciting story, he created a fantasy world with its own creatures, history, mythology, and languages and spoke of the battle between good and evil. Many writers have imitated his style, but none with the same success.

TWAIN, Mark (Samuel Clemens)
1835–1910
U.S. writer

Mark Twain was the pen name used by Samuel Langhorne Clemens, a steamboat pilot on the Mississippi River. He wrote humorous articles for newspapers about the characters he met on his

Two of Mark Twain's most popular books describe life on the Mississippi.

river trips. "Mark twain" was what the sailors shouted when testing the river depth. It means two fathoms (12 feet or about 4 meters) deep.

In 1861, at the start of the Civil War, Twain left the Mississippi and went to look for gold in Nevada, but found none. He traveled abroad and published a witty and successful account of his travels. Twain was soon one of the best-known journalists in the United States. Two favorites among his many books are *Adventures of Tom Sawyer* and *Adventures of Huckleberry Finn*, both based on Twain's memories of his childhood in the country along the Mississippi.

Twain also wrote *A Connecticut Yankee in King Arthur's Court*, a different kind of story. It is the story of a modern man transported back in time to Camelot of long ago. He astonishes King Arthur's court with such marvels as matches, a watch, and gunpowder and is taken for a powerful wizard, a rival to Merlin.

VAN GOGH, Vincent
1853–90
Dutch painter

Van Gogh was the son of a priest, but he knew something of the art world through an uncle who owned an important art gallery. Van Gogh worked there for several years, but then began to study to become a priest. For a while he was a missionary in the coal-mining district of Belgium.

Van Gogh began painting seriously in 1880, when he was 27. At first he painted the peasants, working people, miners, and tramps he had encountered. But then he moved to Paris, where he met French impressionist painters. From there he went to Arles in the south of France. He painted sunny landscapes, orchards, wheatfields, meadows, and vases filled with flowers.

Van Gogh was very bold in his use of dazzling colors, and for extra impact, he would put on the paint with a knife or his fingers, using thick strokes that jutted from the canvas. Some of Van Gogh's pictures from this time (for example *Sunflowers* or *Bridge at Arles*) are among the finest works he ever made, yet in his lifetime he only sold one picture.

All his life, Van Gogh suffered from depression, perhaps because he suffered from epilepsy. In 1888, he had a terrible argument with the French painter Paul Gauguin, who was staying with him at the time. Rather than attack his friend, he turned his anger on himself, and cut off part of his ear.

Soon afterward, convinced that he was a danger to society, he became a voluntary patient in a mental hospital. He spent a year there, creating paintings of chairs, his pipe, his straw hat, and above all, the trees, flowers, and birds of the hospital gardens. But he could find no peace. He died tragically in 1890 at the age of 47.

Vincent Van Gogh was known for his bold use of color.

VERNE, Jules
1828–1905
French writer

Born in Nantes, France, Jules Verne studied to be a lawyer before deciding on a writing career. He became successful with his first novel, *Five Weeks in a Balloon* (1863). After that, his books about fantastic voyages did much to make science fiction a popular new kind of writing.

In his stories, Verne wrote about travel that used forms of transportation not yet invented. These included the submarine and the airplane. He even predicted the space satellite. His best-known books include *A Journey to the Center of the Earth* (1864), *Twenty Thousand Leagues Under the Sea* (1870), and *Around the World in Eighty Days* (1873).

Jules Verne (left) wrote about spaceships and submarines before they were practical.
Laura Ingalls Wilder (below) based her stories on her own life.

WILDER, Laura Ingalls
1867–1957
U.S. writer

Laura Ingalls Wilder was born in Pepin, Wisconsin. She wrote stories about frontier life that were based on her own childhood and growing up in a pioneer family. Her "Little House" books have become children's classics and were the basis for the television series *Little House on the Prairie*. *Little House in the Big Woods* (1932) was the first novel Wilder wrote in a series of nine novels about a family trying to make a home on the American frontier.

In 1954, three years before Wilder's death, the Laura Ingalls Wilder Award was established by a division of the American Library Association. It goes to a writer or illustrator who has made "a lasting and substantial contribution to children's literature." Its first recipient, in 1954, was none other than Laura Ingalls Wilder.

LEADERS

ALEXANDER THE GREAT (Alexandros)
356–323 BC
King of Macedonia (ruled 336-323 BC)

Alexander was born prince of Macedonia, a small, mountainous state now divided among Greece, Bulgaria, and Yugoslavia. His father, Philip the Second, was a warrior who had spent years invading and conquering Greece. When Alexander became King of Macedonia in 336 BC, he made an even bigger plan: to conquer Greece's neighbor, the huge Persian Empire. At that time the empire stretched east from the Mediterranean coast as far as the Ganges River in what is now northern India. This was a distance of more than 2,200 miles (3,500 kilometers).

Alexander began by advancing down the eastern Mediterranean coast as far as Egypt. Then he moved east into Mesopotamia, Babylonia, Parthia, and on toward India.

Wherever he went, he led his troops personally into battle and won tremendous victories. His soldiers compared him to a god, believing that he could not be harmed by humans. Throughout his empire, he set up new towns, run by Greek-speaking commanders and with Greek laws and customs. He named many of them Alexandria after himself. Egypt's chief port, at the mouth of the Nile River, still bears his name.

For over 11 years Alexander the Great led his army in conquests to build his empire. The troops believed he was so powerful that he could not be harmed by humans. Eventually Alexander controlled huge areas of the world.

Alexander's conquests took over 11 years. By the end of that time he controlled huge areas of the world. He wanted to push on further into Asia. His soldiers had always followed him loyally through deserts, over mountains, and into lands said to be the home of giants and cannibals, but now they rebelled against him. They were tired of fighting so far from home. Alexander had little choice but to return to Babylon, the capital of his empire. Before he could reorganize his troops, he became sick (with malaria) and died.

ATTILA
106?–453
King of the Huns (ruled 434-453)

Attila, King of the Huns

In 434 Attila and his brother Bleda inherited the kingdom of the Huns from their uncle. The Huns controlled a huge circle of land centered on what is now Hungary. Attila and Bleda ruled together until 445, when Attila murdered Bleda and became sole king.

At this time the Roman Empire, which had dominated Europe for six centuries, was becoming weak. Attila led his soldiers against one Roman colony after another, pillaging and destroying. He besieged Constantinople, home of the Eastern Roman emperor Theodosius the Second. Attila forced Theodosius to sign a humiliating peace treaty. He then swept west into Gaul (a large part of Western Europe). There he was held back by the skill of the Roman general Aetius and the Vandal chieftain Theodoric.

Attila gathered a new army and in 452 invaded Italy, intending to sack the city of Rome itself. His invasion terrified the Romans because it reminded them of Hannibal's near-fatal advance of 600 years before. According to legend, Pope Leo the First went to Attila and begged him to spare God's holy city. Attila agreed – for a price – and took his armies home. At the same time, his huge army was suffering from famine and disease.

Back in Hungary, Attila began organizing what was to be his biggest invasion so far, that of the Balkans (modern Yugoslavia, Albania, Bulgaria, Romania, and Greece). He saw himself as a second Alexander the Great, and he planned to marry and found a dynasty to rule the world. But on the night of his wedding he died suddenly of a stroke. His generals divided his empire among themselves.

AUGUSTUS
(Gaius Julius Caesar Octavianus)
63 BC–AD 14
Roman emperor (ruled 27 BC-AD 14)

Octavianus was Julius Caesar's great-nephew, and he was eventually adopted by Caesar as his son and heir in 44 BC. He supported Caesar against Pompey in the Roman civil war, and for 17 years after Caesar's death, he fought for power with other leading Romans, including Mark Antony.

Until this time, the Romans had been ruled by the Senate, or council of leading citizens. They hated the idea of any one person gaining unlimited power. For this reason, Octavianus called himself Princeps ("Principal Senator"), not "President" or "King." The Senate gave him the title of Augustus ("Serene Highness").

In 27 BC, Augustus became Rome's first emperor. Although he claimed to bow to the Senate's will, he kept two powers that gave him sole rule. One allowed him to propose new laws and to forbid any laws he did not like. Another gave him supreme command of the army in peace and war.

If Augustus had been a tyrant, no one would have supported him for long. But his rule was orderly, generous, and fair – a welcome relief after nearly 50 years of civil war. Augustus reorganized the government, the army, the law courts, and the tax system. He rebuilt Rome's main buildings in marble. He also paid such authors as Virgil and Livy to write works glorifying the Roman people. Augustus ruled as emperor of Rome from 27 BC until his death in AD 14.

BISMARCK, Otto Eduard Leopold von
1815–98
German political leader

Bismarck was a Prussian nobleman who was a lawyer by profession. He entered politics in 1847 and was known for his excellent speeches. Bismarck's greatest ambition was to unite the separate German states into one country. In 1871, Germany was united after a long series of wars with Denmark, Austria, and France. Bismarck was made chancellor (political leader) of the new empire.

Bismarck's rule was strict, earning him the nickname of the "Iron Chancellor." He believed in protecting wealthy landowners and passed laws to limit the power of the growing merchant class.

While Wilhelm the First was kaiser (emperor) of Germany, Bismarck's ideas were widely used. But when Wilhelm the Second came to power in 1888, Bismarck's influence began to fade. In 1890, he was dismissed from the government. He retired and took no further part in politics.

Bismarck was known as the "Iron Chancellor" because of his determination to unify Germany.

CAESAR, Gaius Julius
100–44 BC
Roman general and political leader

When Caesar was 23 he was kidnapped by pirates and held for ransom. As soon as the ransom money was paid, he gathered an army, rounded up the pirates, and killed them. Then he used the ransom money to pay his soldiers. By this one daring stroke he made himself a general with a private army loyal to him rather than to the people of Rome. For the rest of his life, his loyal troops let him do pretty much as he pleased, although he was officially a state servant.

Caesar fought Rome's enemies brilliantly. He was especially successful in Gaul (a large part of Western Europe) and Spain. But his main interest was political power in Rome. He formed an alliance with two other leading Romans – the banker Crassus and Pompey, another general – to bypass the Senate (the governing body in Rome) and run state affairs.

At first the "triumvirate" (three-person alliance), as it was called, worked well, but each member was ambitious, and they soon argued. Crassus faded from power, and Pompey and Caesar were at each other's throats. Their quarrel led to civil war in 49 BC.

Caesar finally defeated Pompey at the battle of Pharsalus in 48 BC, and the panic-stricken Senate made him dictator (sole ruler), hoping that this would keep him under their orders. But Caesar's supporters began saying that the name he really deserved was "king," and it was obvious that he had the power to take that title any time he chose. A group of senators, led by Brutus and Cassius, plotted to murder Caesar, and on the Ides (15th) of March, 44 BC, they stabbed him dead at the feet of Pompey's statue in the Senate.

Julius Caesar was the greatest general of his time. He ruled Rome with two other generals. While Caesar went off to conquer Gaul (France) the other two remained behind and ruled Rome.

CAROLVS ○ MAGNVS

Charlemagne was king of the Franks (French) from 768 to 814. He was a great admirer of learning. He founded a school and encouraged literature and the arts.

CHARLEMAGNE
742–814
Emperor of the West (ruled 768-814)

The name Charlemagne is made from three medieval French words meaning "Charles the Great." Charlemagne became the sole king of the Franks (a people inhabiting most of modern France and Belgium) in 771 when his brother died, and set about conquering neighboring peoples to the east, north, and south. He added vast new lands to his empire, conquering most of what are now Germany, Austria, the Netherlands, Switzerland, and northern Italy.

In 800, Pope Leo the Third crowned Charlemagne "emperor of the West" – an ancient Roman title that made him the successor of the Roman emperors.

Charlemagne wanted to create one single, united empire, not a collection of different states. He proclaimed the whole empire Christian, and it later became known as the Holy Roman Empire.

Charlemagne built new churches and monasteries everywhere. In addition, he standardized the laws and sent imperial officials and soldiers to ensure that they were obeyed. He encouraged his nobles to learn to read and write. He set an example himself by learning to read (although not to write) and to speak Latin and Greek. Furthermore, he asked the scholar Alcuin to plan an education system gathering the best ideas of both his own time and the past.

Charlemagne also built roads and aqueducts throughout the empire.

Charlemagne's ambition was to restore the glory of the ancient Roman Empire – and while he lived, he succeeded. Writers of his time tell of a noble, powerful prince surrounded by a glittering court and devoted to religious glory, honesty, and truth. Unfortunately for Europe, Charlemagne's successors were not as talented as he was. They fought over the empire and divided it – and Europe has remained a collection of separate, often fighting, countries ever since.

CHURCHILL, Sir Winston Leonard Spencer
1874–1965
English political leader and writer

Churchill began his career as a soldier. In 1899 he went to South Africa as a war reporter, sending news to a London newspaper about the Boer War that was being fought there. When he returned to England, he began a career in politics and in 1900 he was elected to Parliament. From 1911 to 1915, after World War One began, he was the First Lord of the Admiralty, in charge of Britain's navy.

In the 1920s, Churchill disagreed more and more with his fellow politicians. He disliked the way they were handing over British power in India. Later he became more worried than they were about the growing power of Germany's Adolf Hitler in Europe. Churchill retired to his country house, where he spent most of the 1930s writing books (mostly on history) and painting. But in 1939, when Parliament at last realized that fighting Hitler was the only way to stop him from taking over Europe, Churchill returned to politics. In 1940 he was made prime minister.

Churchill led the British people throughout World War Two. He inspired them to fight by his own personal courage and by making magnificent speeches. Many of the these were recorded and can still be heard.

After the war there was an election, and

Winston Churchill led Great Britain through World War Two. He was a soldier, statesman, and writer. His speeches and courage inspired the country. Here, he holds up his fingers in the famous "V for victory" sign.

Churchill's Conservative Party lost. But in 1951 it returned to power, and Churchill was prime minister until 1955. He went on working and writing until he was over 85. When he died, at age 90, he was given a state funeral.

CLEOPATRA
69–30 BC
Egyptian queen (ruled 51-30 BC)

Known as one of the most beautiful women in the world, Cleopatra ruled Egypt for more than twenty years. She used her beauty to attract some of the most powerful men of her time, including Julius Caesar.

When Caesar was assassinated, Cleopatra joined forces with his old friend, Mark Antony. Together they fought against Octavian who was to have been Caesar's heir. In the battle of Actium in 31 BC, Cleopatra's and Antony's forces were defeated.

Rather than submit to Octavian, Cleopatra killed herself. According to legend, she did this by letting a poisonous snake bite her. The story of these events is told in Shakespeare's play, *Antony and Cleopatra.*

A statue of Cleopatra, which was presented to Juba the Second, king of Algeria, during her lifetime. It was a true likeness of the queen, unlike many images made of her.

ELIZABETH the First
1533–1603
English queen (ruled 1558-1603)

Elizabeth was the youngest surviving child of King Henry the Eighth. During the reign of Mary, her elder sister, England was brought to the edge of financial and political ruin. This was partly because of wars against the French and partly because of fighting in England itself, between Protestants and Catholics.

In 1558, when Elizabeth succeeded her older sister Mary as Queen, she quickly made peace with France. But she refused to keep England Catholic, as it had been under Mary. This angered the Catholic kings of Spain. The Spaniards were also angered by the way Elizabeth refused to punish Sir Walter Raleigh, Sir Francis Drake, and other English sea captains for attacking Spanish ships and settlements in the New World. Finally in 1588, King Philip the Second of Spain sent a huge armada (armed fleet) to attack Britain. Some of the ships were destroyed by the British. Some were blown off-course by storms and sunk. The armada was no longer a threat, although the war between Spain and England dragged on for years.

Elizabeth never married. Her long reign restored the prosperity England had lost in Mary's time and gave it back the glory it had known under Henry the Eighth. Queen Elizabeth favored writers and musicians and encouraged explorers and adventurers. British people still look back on her reign, the time of writers such as William Shakespeare, as one of the most glittering periods of their history.

Elizabeth the First is shown here with symbols representing her achievements during her reign. The ships are the fleet that she sent out to defend Britain against the Spanish, and to conquer new territories. She has her hand on a globe to symbolize the discoveries made by her explorers in the New World.

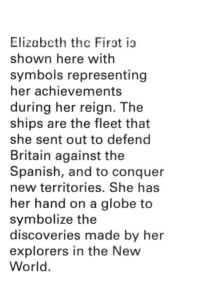

GANDHI, Mohandas Karamchand
1869–1948
Leader of independence for India

Gandhi started his career as a lawyer, working in London and Bombay, and then for 21 years in South Africa. In 1915, he went home to India to win political rights for members of the Hindu faith known as the "untouchables." These were members of the lowest class of society, who were regarded as outcasts by other followers of the religion. Soon he began a second political struggle – to win India freedom from British imperial rule.

Mohandas Gandhi was considered by some people to be a kind of holy man. People gave him the name *Mahatma*, which means "Great Soul."

Instead of using force in the independence struggle, Gandhi preferred "non-cooperation." He and his followers refused to pay taxes to the British, to have their children educated in British-run schools, or to buy British goods.

Although the authorities regarded Gandhi as a nuisance most people treated him as a kind of holy man. They called him *Mahatma* ("Great Soul") and gathered in millions to hear him speak.

Eventually, in 1944, the British were prepared to hold serious independence talks. By now Gandhi foresaw new dangers: that Hindus and Muslims would fight each other after independence, and that India would be torn by civil war. There was even talk of a new state, Pakistan, which would be Muslim while the rest of India was Hindu. Gandhi preached that all people should live in peace and that there should be no barriers between them. But the authorities went ahead regardless. India and a new nation, Pakistan, were declared separate states in 1947 – and rioting broke out. At one riot, in Delhi in 1948, Gandhi was trying to stop people from fighting when he was killed by an assassin.

GENGHIS KHAN (Temujin)
1162–1227
Mongol emperor (ruled 1206-27)

When Temujin was a boy, his father, a chief of the Mongols, died. Temujin inherited his father's title. He became chief of a warrior tribe in Mongolia, part of the borderland between modern China and the Soviet Union. He set about conquering all the neighboring tribes, and finally ruled so many people that he was given the title *Genghis Khan* ("universal ruler") in 1206.

Genghis Khan's army consisted of ferocious and merciless horsemen. They swarmed over the Great Wall of China, overran northern China and Korea, and streamed into the countries now known as the Soviet Union, Iran, and Pakistan. Wherever a town or city opposed him, Genghis Khan destroyed it and killed its people.

By the time Genghis Khan died, he ruled an empire stretching over 3,750 miles (6,000 kilometers) from the Pacific Ocean in the east to the Caspian Sea in the west. His soldiers carried his body in state to his capital city, Karakorum, in Mongolia. His sons quarreled over who should succeed him, and it was not until 1259, 32 years later, that Genghis Khan's grandson, Kublai Khan, restored firm rule.

GORBACHEV, Mikhail Sergeevich
1931–
Soviet leader

Born in the village of Privolnoye, Gorbachev studied law and attended an agricultural college

Mikhail Gorbachev has introduced many changes in the way the Soviet Union is run. For his efforts, he was awarded the 1990 Nobel Peace Prize.

before taking on increasingly important roles in the Communist Party. He became leader of the U.S.S.R. in 1985 and was appointed president in 1988. He started to reform the systems of government and business in his country to make them more efficient and helpful to the people. His economic reform policy became known as *perestroika*. He also encouraged a policy of *glasnost* ("openness"): it means that people should be told what is happening and should have a say in their own lives.

HENRY the Eighth
1491–1547
English king (ruled 1509-47)

One of the most strong-willed kings to sit on the English throne, Henry the Eighth is best known for his conflict with the Roman Catholic Church and for his six wives. Henry's first wife, Catherine of Aragon, bore him five children, but the only one to survive was a girl, Mary. Wanting a male heir, Henry decided to divorce Catherine and to take a new queen, Anne Boleyn.

Because he was a Roman Catholic, Henry was forbidden to divorce unless the Pope agreed. He tried unsuccessfully for years to persuade the Pope to let him divorce Catherine. In 1533, he announced that the Church of England would be entirely separate from the Roman Catholic Church. He also announced that he, not the Pope, would be its head. Henry then divorced Catherine and married Anne.

To Henry's fury, Anne Boleyn produced no sons. Her only surviving child was a daughter, Elizabeth. In 1536, Henry had Anne beheaded because he thought she was unfaithful to him.

Henry married four more times. Jane Seymour did provide him with a son and heir (later King Edward the Sixth), but Jane died in childbirth. Henry then married Anne of Cleves, a German princess, but divorced her after a few months. Catherine Howard, his fifth wife, was accused of being unfaithful to him, and Henry had her executed. Catherine Parr, who married Henry when he was old and sick, survived him.

Despite his marriages and treatment of his wives, Henry the Eighth was considered a charming, witty man. He was also popular with his people. But he could be and often was ruthless, imprisoning or murdering those who opposed him. Henry's reign lasted from 1509 to 1547, the year of his death. His political and military strength laid the foundation for the successful reign of his daughter, Elizabeth the First.

Henry the Eighth had six wives. He is pictured here with two of them – Anne Boleyn and Catherine Parr.

HITLER, Adolf
1889–1945
German dictator (ruled 1933-45)

In the early 1920s, Hitler joined the tiny National Socialist German Workers' Party (Nazi party), an extreme right-wing group. He spent the next 10 years building the Nazi party into one of the largest political parties in Germany.

In 1923, Hitler led an unsuccessful Nazi revolution to take over the province of Bavaria. He was sent to prison for treason. While there, he wrote *Mein Kampf* ("My Struggle"), which outlined his plans for the German conquest of Europe and his hatred for the Jews.

Adolf Hitler ruled Germany as a dictator from 1933 to 1945. He started World War Two. It took the combined forces of the United States, Britain, the Soviet Union, and many other nations to stop him. A Nazi political rally is shown above.

In 1932 Hitler ran as a candidate in the German presidential election, but he lost. One year later, a new election was held and the Nazis gained control. From then on, Hitler was all-powerful. He proclaimed himself Führer ("leader") and abolished all opposing political parties. He created a force of secret police, the Gestapo, and spoke of Germany's great future.

By 1936 all Germany was under Hitler's spell. He began building up the army, navy, and air force. He announced that soon Germany would conquer the world. In 1939 his troops invaded Poland and Czechoslovakia. Britain and France declared war on Germany, signaling the start of World War Two.

By 1944, after millions had been killed on all sides, it was clear that Germany's opponents, the Allies, were winning. They took back country after country from the Nazis. In 1945 they began advancing through Germany itself, and in April the Allied forces reached Berlin. Hitler died less than two weeks before Germany surrendered.

After the war, the leading Nazis were put on trial at Nuremberg. The details of their crimes horrified the world. The world learned that over six million Jews, gypsies, communists, and others had been killed in concentration camps. This terrible slaughter is now known as the "Holocaust." Even more than his political plotting or the destructive war he began, this crime is what makes people remember Hitler with hatred.

JACKSON, Andrew
1767–1845
7th U.S. President (in office 1829-37)

Andrew Jackson believed in the common man. Perhaps this was because he came from humble beginnings. He was born in a log cabin on a farm in the Carolinas. His father died a few days before Jackson's birth, leaving his mother to raise three boys. At the age of 13 Jackson fought with South Carolina forces against the British in the American Revolution. He was captured, put in prison, and then released.

At about this time Jackson's mother died. Not long after, he started studying law and passed the law examinations in 1787.

In 1788 Jackson settled in what became the state of Tennessee in 1796. He married in 1791 and earned his living by dabbling in law, growing cotton, owning a store, and speculating in real estate.

Jackson was elected to Congress. He served as a Representative from Tennessee (1796-97) and as a Senator (1797-98).

At the start of the War of 1812, Jackson was commissioned a general in the U.S. Army. He was charged with protecting the city of New Orleans in Louisiana. In the Battle of New Orleans (1815), U.S. troops successfully drove off the attacking British.

Because of his military successes, people thought that Jackson should be president. He briefly returned to the Senate and from there was nominated for the presidency. In 1824 he won the popular vote but lost the election because the vote had to be decided by the House of Representatives. In 1828, more people voted, and more voted for Jackson. He, at long last, had become president.

Jackson was accused of initiating the spoils system – appointing supporters to positions in the government. Jackson maintained, however, that as long as a person was capable of doing a job, it did no harm to appoint one to whom a favor was owed. During his administration he also ordered the resettlement of Indians who lived in the East. Lands were put aside for this purpose in the western territory. White settlers were in favor of this, but it was not good for the Indians.

Jackson was reelected in 1832. He did not run again, wishing only to retire to the Hermitage, the house he had built in 1819 in Nashville, Tennessee. He is buried on its grounds.

JEFFERSON, Thomas
1743–1826
3rd U.S. president (in office 1801-09)

Although Jefferson was known as a lawyer and politician, he had many other skills. He spoke several languages, including Latin, Greek, and French, and had a good knowledge of math, science, and history. He designed his own house, Monticello, and much of his furniture, including a chair that revolved to follow the sunlight, and a four-sided music stand that allowed string-quartet players to sit in a circle and see each other as they played.

Jefferson went into politics at 26, and almost at once began working to win American independence from British rule. He served on the committee assigned to draft the Declaration of Independence. Although a few changes were made after it was finished, the Declaration is almost entirely Jefferson's work.

The first draft of the Declaration of Independence was made by Thomas Jefferson. He was a delegate to the Continental Congress of the thirteen American colonies in 1776.

During the American Revolution Jefferson served in Congress and as governor of Virginia, from 1779 to 1781. He was the first Secretary of State for the new republic, in charge of foreign affairs, under President George Washington. In 1796 he was elected vice president. After serving under President John Adams, Jefferson was elected president in 1800. During his administration the U.S. government made the Louisiana Purchase in 1803, buying a vast area of North America from Napoleon the First at less than four cents per acre. He also abolished the slave trade with Africa and planned and organized the Lewis and Clark expedition to explore America's Far West.

Jefferson was reelected in 1804 and retired in 1809. He spent his last years working for the University of Virginia at Charlottesville. He raised money to found it, designed the buildings and furniture, and chose the subjects to be taught. He died on July 4, 1826, the same day as John Adams.

JOSEPH, Chief
1840–1904
Indian leader

Joseph was born in the Wallowa Valley in what is now the state of Oregon. His father was the chief of the Nez Perce Indians. (*Nez Perce* is French for

Chief Joseph led the Indian people in the
northwestern United States.

"pierced nose.") When his father died, Joseph became the chief.

In 1855, the Nez Perce Indians agreed to give
some of their land in the northwest to the U.S.
Government in exchange for keeping some land in
what is now Oregon and Idaho. When gold was discovered in 1863 on the Nez Perce's land in Oregon,
the U.S. Government tried to take that land, too.
The younger Nez Perce braves, led by Joseph,
fought to keep their land and won several victories
over the U.S. Army.

The forces against the Nez Perce Indians were
too strong, however. And so Chief Joseph retreated
and tried to lead his people to Canada. They were
almost at the Canadian border when they were
overtaken by U.S. troops. Because of the weak con-
dition of his people, Joseph surrendered. He and
his people were first sent to an Indian reservation
in Oklahoma and then, in 1883, to Idaho. Finally,
they were sent to Washington, where Chief Joseph
died.

KHOMEINI, Ayatollah Ruhollah
1900?–89
Iranian religious leader (in office 1979-89)

Ruhollah Moussavi grew up in Khomein, Persia
(now Iran). As a young man he took the last name
of Khomeini from the name of his hometown.
Later, as an Islamic scholar, he was given the title
"Ayatollah," which means "reflection of God" and
is given to those who are leaders in the Shi'ite Muslim religion.

As a teacher of religion, the ayatollah often criticized the leader of Iran, Shah Mohammed Riza
Pahlávi. He felt that the shah was not keeping to
the rules of the Muslim religion and was being influenced by the outside world.

The shah put the ayatollah in prison in 1963 and
then made him leave Iran in 1964. The ayatollah
went first to Iraq and then to Paris, France. He was
still able to direct his people from these foreign
places and he encouraged them to overthrow the
shah. When riots broke out during a strike, the
shah himself left the country, and Ayatollah Khomeini was able to return to Iran in 1979.

Named "ruler for life," the ayatollah isolated his
country from the outside world and urged strict ad-
herence to the Muslim laws. Any of his followers
who disobeyed his rules were severely punished –
even executed.

Iran's Ayatollah
Khomeini thought
people were ignoring
God. Khomeini was in
Paris when the shah of
Iran was driven out, and
he returned to Iran after
the revolution.

KUBLAI KHAN
1216–94
Mongol emperor (ruled 1259-94)

Kublai Khan, the grandson of the Mongolian
emperor Genghis Khan, ruled over an empire that
stretched from the Black Sea to the Pacific Ocean.
His first capital city was Karakorum in Mongolia.
During his reign, he ordered a magnificent new
capital city to be built at Cambaluc, which is now
modern day Beijing in China.

Kublai Khan spent much of his reign conquering
or keeping peaceful the southern regions of his
empire – modern Afghanistan, Tibet, and Burma.
The only nearby places he failed to conquer were
Japan and Java. The attempt failed mostly
because his invasion force of 140,000 men was destroyed in a storm at sea.

Kublai Khan's power depended on his soldiers,
who were among the most terrifying in all world
history. Kublai Khan's rule from 1259 to 1294,
however, was mostly generous and fair. He ordered
roads to be built throughout his empire and estab-

lished a large system of waterways to transport grain across China.

Unlike previous rulers, Kublai Khan allowed freedom of religion and encouraged trade with foreigners. The Venetian merchant Marco Polo spent 17 years in Kublai Khan's service and wrote a famous account of the empire and court.

LEE, Robert Edward
1807–70
U.S. military leader

Robert E. Lee was born into a famous Virginia military family. His father was General Henry "Light-Horse Harry" Lee, one of George Washington's officers and a governor of Virginia. In 1825 Robert E. Lee entered the U.S. Military Academy at West Point. Four years later he graduated with high honors, second in his class. As a second lieutenant, he began his service in the army in the Corps of Engineers.

He worked at establishing boundaries and at developing harbors. In 1846, at the start of the Mexican War, he supervised the building of bridges in Texas. He fought bravely throughout the war.

Robert Edward Lee was the commander of the Confederate forces during the U.S. Civil War. He led an army of about 75,000 men.

From 1852 until 1855 he was superintendent of the military academy at West Point. In 1855, by now a lieutenant colonel, he commanded troops on the Texas frontier. On a visit to Washington, D.C., he became involved in restoring order after the raid on Harpers Ferry by John Brown in 1859.

When the Southern states left the Union in 1861 over the question of slavery, Lee at first did not know what to do. He had served the Union well, and he loved his country. He also loved his home state of Virginia, even though he had never believed in slavery. When he had inherited the family slaves, he had let them go free. Now, after much thought, Lee felt that he had to stand by Virginia. He resigned from the Union army and went home to serve in the Confederate Army in the Civil War. Soon after he was made a general.

At the Battle of Fair Oaks (Seven Pines) in 1862, Lee became commander of the Army of Northern Virginia. His army was able to hold off Union forces during several battles in 1862. Then Lee's troops won at Fredericksburg and at Chancellorsville, both in Virginia, but they were defeated at Gettysburg, as they moved into Pennsylvania. In 1864, the Confederates were badly defeated in the Wilderness campaign and the Union army captured Richmond, Virginia, in 1865. Worn out, Lee's army surrendered at Appomattox Court House, Virginia, on April 9, 1865. The Civil War was over.

Later in 1865, when Lee entered private life, he took the job of president of Washington College, a small college in Lexington, Virginia. He worked hard to improve the course of study and to expand the campus. After 1870, the school was renamed Washington and Lee University. Lee is buried in a chapel on the campus grounds.

LENIN, Vladimir Ilyich
1870–1924
Russian leader

When Lenin (originally called Vladimir Ilyich Ulyanov) was a student, he read the works of Karl Marx, the founder of modern communism. He made up his mind to end the harsh rule of the Tsars (Russian kings) and other rich and powerful people. He wanted to give political power to the peasants and workers. In the 1890s he joined the newly formed Social Democratic Party, which was based on the ideas of Marx. Soon he became the leader of one of its main groups, the Bolsheviks ("majority").

Lenin, the Russian Revolutionary leader, speaking in Moscow. Just beneath him is Trotsky who became leader of the Red Army. Lenin is a national hero in the U.S.S.R. His statue is in every town and there are paintings or photographs of him in every public building.

In 1905 the Bolsheviks organized strikes and demonstrations against the government. These grew into a revolution, which the government managed to stop. Lenin lived in Switzerland and other parts of Europe until February 1917, when there was a second revolution in Russia. The Tsar was removed from power, and it was safe for Lenin to return home. For several months there was a power struggle between the army, the old government officials, and the revolutionaries led by Lenin. Finally, in October 1917, the Bolsheviks won control.

The next few years were very hard for Lenin. No one had ever before created an entirely Marxist state. The Bolsheviks planned to take over all privately owned land and businesses. They would then redistribute them to all the people ("shared ownership" or "communism"). Not surprisingly, the original owners fought this plan. A civil war began and millions of people died or left the country before the Bolsheviks won in 1920. There was hunger, poverty, and misery even greater than before the Revolution. But at last, the new political system was established. The Union of Soviet Socialist Republics (U.S.S.R.), the largest country in the world, united 15 communist republics. Each of these was led by a "soviet" or workers' congress.

In 1922, Lenin suffered a stroke, and 18 months later he died. His body was preserved and placed in a huge tomb in Moscow's Red Square. His statues stood in every town. Paintings or photographs of him were in every public building. He was honored throughout the U.S.S.R. as the nation's founding father.

LINCOLN, Abraham
1809–65
16th U.S. president (in office 1861-65)

Lincoln grew up in the wilderness of Kentucky and Indiana. There were few books and schools, so he taught himself. Eventually he became a lawyer and was elected to Congress in 1846. In 1856 he joined the Republican Party, which had been formed two years earlier to fight slavery. In 1860 he was elected U.S. president.

All through the 1850s the north and the south argued fiercely about slavery. The northern states were against it; the southern states approved of it. Shortly after Lincoln became president, the southerners declared themselves a separate country with a government and laws of their own. Lincoln ordered troops into action to prevent this, and the southern army fought back. In 1861 the Civil War began.

The Civil War looked as if it would destroy the United States. But throughout the fighting, Lincoln spoke hopefully about the future. He said that as soon as the war was over, he would "bind up the nation's wounds." In one of his best-known speeches, honoring soldiers killed at Gettysburg in 1863, he called democracy the best form of rule – government "of the people, by the people, and for the people." In 1864 he was elected for four more years as president; in 1865 the south surrendered (gave up) and the Civil War was over.

Lincoln now faced the hardest task of his whole presidency: to make friends of people who had wanted to fight each other only days before. But only five days after the surrender, he was shot to death in a theater by the actor John Wilkes Booth. His death shocked the nation.

Abraham Lincoln was the 16th President of the United States. He kept the country together during the Civil War, which lasted from 1861 to 1865. He was an opponent of slavery and issued the Emancipation Proclamation in 1863 to try to end it.

LOUIS the Fourteenth
1638–1715
French king (ruled 1643-1715)

Louis inherited the French throne when he was only four years old. During his childhood, there was an ongoing argument between his mother, who ruled on his behalf, and the parliament of nobles who wanted a share of power. When Louis was old enough to take control, he disbanded parliament and said that he would be the only power in the land. He met every morning with a group of advisers, and between them they decided everything that should be done.

Louis ordered a magnificent palace to be built at Versailles. It was the biggest and most spectacular structure in Europe. He ruled there in such splendor that people nicknamed him "the Sun King." Artists, musicians, writers, and thinkers came to Versailles, where Louis supported them.

As Louis grew old, his nobles began to plot against him, and other European nations made alliances against the French. Only Louis's political skill kept his kingdom from falling apart.

When Louis was 64, he declared war on Spain, trying to win the Spanish throne for his grandson, Philip. The 11 years of fighting that followed were known as the "War of the Spanish Succession." The war left France very weak.

Besides this public disaster, Louis suffered private grief. His sons and grandsons – his heirs – died one by one. Soon, he had no one to leave the

French throne to except his great-grandson, a child of only five. It is one reason why his reign as king was the longest in modern European history – an amazing 72 years, from 1643 to his death in 1715.

MAO ZEDONG (Mao Tse-tung)
1893–1976
Chinese leader (ruled 1949-76)

Until Mao Zedong was 28, he worked as a librarian. Attracted to communism in 1918, he helped to found the Chinese Communist Party in 1921. At that time, communists all over the world were excited by the success of the Russian Revolution (see Lenin). Mao wanted to lead a workers' revolution in China, too. The Nationalist Party, which disagreed with Mao, violently attacked communist ideas. When he set up the first Chinese Marxist state, in the southern province of Jiangxi (Kiangsi), insults turned to war. Led by Chiang Kai-shek (Jiang Jieshi), the nationalists sent soldiers to kill every communist they could find.

By 1934 Mao's enemies were ready for a final attack. His followers seemed doomed. But he decided on a daring escape plan. He took a huge group of people and set out to walk to safety.

The "Long March," as it came to be called, lasted for 12 months and covered 6,000 miles (9,700 kilometers). The marchers climbed mountains and crossed deserts and rivers. They were attacked at every step by Chiang Kai-shek's soldiers. They survived only because of the kindness of people they met on the way. In the end, 30,000 survivors reached safety in Yan'an (Yenan) and set up new homes there.

Throughout this time of civil war, the Japanese had been taking control of Chinese territory in the east. By 1938 it was clear that World War Two was about to start in Europe. The Japanese – as allies (partners) of Germany – wanted to take advantage of the civil war to take over China.

Faced with this danger, the Chinese communists and nationalists made peace long enough to fight

Louis the Fourteenth of France was known as "the Sun King." He ordered a magnificent palace (below) to be built at Versailles, in France.

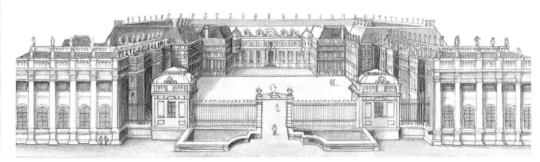

Mao Zedong resigned the chairmanship of the party in 1959, but retained his chairmanship of the party Politburo until he died in 1976. After his death, many of his most trusted advisors, including his wife, were arrested and stood trial.

Napoleon the First was emperor of the French between 1804 and 1814. As well as leading military action, he reorganized the French government, the law, and the Bank of France. The shaded area in the map above shows the parts of Europe over which Napoleon or his candidates ruled at the height of his power.

the Japanese. But in 1946, as soon as World War Two was over and Germany and Japan had lost, the Chinese civil war broke out again. The United States supported Chiang Kai-shek and the nationalists. The Soviet Union supported Mao and the communists.

After three years of fighting, the nationalists lost. The communist People's Republic of China was born with Mao as its first leader. In 1958 he tried to improve production on farms and in factories. But this program, called the Great Leap Forward, failed. In the early 1960s, he argued with the officials of the Soviet Union about who was the leader of the communist world. He did unite the Chinese people and improve their lives, providing better homes, food, and jobs.

Although Mao is best known as a political and military leader, he was also a writer. Most of his works are political. They describe how he thought Marx's communist ideas should be changed for the needs of the Chinese people. But he also wrote poems about the seasons and the beauty of nature, love, and friendship.

NAPOLEON the First
1769–1821
French emperor (ruled 1799-1814; 1815)

Napoleon Bonaparte was educated in military schools and became an army officer. As a young man he sided with the French revolutionaries. He later led the French army against the Austrians and the British, who wanted to crush the revolution and bring back royal rule. His only defeat during these 10 years of campaigning was at the battle of the Nile in 1798, when the British under Horatio Nelson destroyed the French fleet. Napoleon slipped back to France. By this time the members of the Directory (the French revolutionary government) were arguing among themselves.

In 1799 Napoleon led a revolt against them and seized power.

Napoleon wanted to make France the center of a huge European empire, modeled on ancient Rome. He formed a senate with himself as first consul. In 1804 he crowned himself emperor. He organized French laws in the same way as Rome's had been. He built a network of roads and bridges to give his army access to trouble spots anywhere in France. He signed a treaty with the British to get his soldiers back from Egypt. Then almost at once he began attacking neighboring countries, hoping to add all Europe to his empire.

As an army commander, Napoleon was a genius. But although he conquered the huge Austrian Empire, and for a few years ruled Italy, Switzerland, and Germany, he found the rest of Europe more than a match for him. The British navy sank his fleet at Trafalgar in 1805. On land the Spanish and Portuguese, helped by soldiers from many other European nations, kept his army pinned down for over six years. This was called "The Peninsular War."

Napoleon turned to eastern Europe, and led over

half a million men into Russia. He entered Moscow in 1812, but found that nearly all its citizens had fled. Fires broke out all over the city and left it all but destroyed. With no place to house his soldiers and no food for them to eat, Napoleon was forced to retreat. His soldiers were unprepared for the terrible Russian winter, and over 400,000 died.

Seeing Napoleon's army so weak, the European states started a united attack. In 1813 they defeated Napoleon at Leipzig and the next year sent him to the tiny Mediterranean island of Elba. In 1815 he escaped, went back to France, and declared himself emperor once again. He ruled for 100 days, while the Europeans gathered their armies for a battle that would end his reign for good. This came in 1815, at Waterloo. Napoleon was sent into exile once again, this time to the far away Atlantic island of St. Helena, where he remained until his death.

PETER the First ("the Great")
1672–1725
Russian emperor (ruled 1682-1725)

The sixteenth and seventeenth centuries were the great age of exploration and discovery in Europe. Russia, however, had remained an isolated, backward country. The Russians had stayed in their own vast lands, avoiding contact with outsiders. Europeans traveled west to the New World of the Americas, or south to Africa and India. Very few went east to visit Russia.

Peter the Great modernized his backward country and made it a strong nation. He toured Europe and invited westerners to visit Russia.

Peter wanted to end his country's isolation. He toured foreign countries to see how things were done in the West. Western writers, artists, and thinkers were invited to Russia, and foreign books were translated into Russian. The power of the Russian nobles was reduced. The country was reorganized on the model of such Western monarchies as England, France, and Sweden. Russian industry was modernized. New methods of farming and textile manufacturing were introduced.

The emperor's reforms did not please everyone in Russia, particularly the nobles whose power he was reducing. In 1698 there was a revolt, which he crushed without mercy. He used the newly modernized army and navy to protect Russia's borders, like fighting the Swedes for access to the Baltic Sea. He moved Russia's capital from Moscow to a magnificent new city on the Baltic. He called the new city St. Petersburg (now Leningrad). He filled it with buildings like those at Versailles, the palace of Louis the Fourteenth of France.

ROOSEVELT, Franklin Delano
1882–1945
32nd U.S. president (in office 1933-45)

Roosevelt, a lawyer, went into politics in his mid-twenties and was elected a state senator. He then rose quickly to high office, serving as assistant secretary for the navy for seven years and running unsuccessfully for election as vice president. Then, in 1921, he was struck by polio and became crippled from the waist down. This would have ended many people's careers. But Roosevelt began a daily routine of physical therapy to make his muscles as healthy as possible. This routine was so successful that he was able to appear in public without many people even knowing that he was paralyzed. He was elected governor of New York State in 1928 and president of the United States in 1932.

In the early 1930s the United States was in crisis. After the 1929 "Wall Street Crash," when the American stock market collapsed, companies were going out of business all over the country. Millions of people were unemployed, and there was no welfare system. Despair and misery were everywhere. Roosevelt fought the Depression, as it was called, with what he termed a "New Deal." He

Franklin Delano Roosevelt was the only person in the United States ever to be elected president four times. He guided the U.S.A. through both the Depression and World War Two.

poured government money into building dams, irrigation projects, roads, city centers, and houses. The construction companies had jobs to offer the unemployed. Recovering from the Depression took years, but by the end of the 1930s the New Deal had worked. The United States was prosperous again.

In 1939, when World War Two began, Roosevelt at first kept the United States out of the fighting. Then, in 1941, the Japanese (allies of the Germans and the Italians) bombed the U.S. fleet in Pearl Harbor, Hawaii. Roosevelt called the attack "a day that will live in infamy" and the United States declared war. American money, soldiers, and weapons were sent to help the European countries opposed to Hitler, and U.S. forces fought the Japanese in the Pacific.

All through the war, in stirring public speeches, many of them filmed for newsreels, and in radio "fireside chats," Roosevelt tirelessly encouraged the Americans to fight for freedom as they had fought in the Depression for prosperity. His wife Eleanor made many public appearances to help the war effort. By the end of the fighting, she was recognized and loved all across the country.

Roosevelt died in 1945, only three weeks before the end of the war in Europe. He was the only person in U.S. history to be elected president four times.

ROOSEVELT, Theodore
1858–1919
26th U.S. President (in office 1901-09)

Roosevelt was born of wealthy parents in New York City.

After graduation from Harvard in 1880, Roosevelt became interested in politics. He served in the New York State Legislature for three years. After the deaths of his wife and his mother in 1884, he decided to raise cattle at a ranch in the West. He had always wanted to be a cowboy. He stayed for two years. Upon his return, he married again.

A Republican, Roosevelt served on the U.S. Civil Service Commission from 1889. In 1897, he became assistant secretary of the navy.

Roosevelt resigned from the Navy Department in 1898 so that he could fight in the Spanish-American War. He went to Cuba to command a cavalry unit. His unit was nicknamed the Rough Riders because of their bravery in the taking of San Juan Hill in Santiago, Cuba.

Riding on his popularity, Roosevelt was elected governor of New York in 1898. In 1900 he became vice president of the United States. When President McKinley died from an assassin's bullet in 1901, Roosevelt became the president. He was the youngest man ever to hold this office.

As president, Roosevelt believed that everybody deserved to be treated fairly. He initiated the Square Deal and he fought for the rights of the ordinary people.

Roosevelt also believed that the United States should help protect the other countries in the Western hemisphere.

During Roosevelt's administration, the Panama Canal was built. An enthusiastic conservationist, he saw that western lands could be used for farming. For his help in bringing about a peace to the war between the Russians and the Japanese in 1905, he was awarded the 1906 Nobel Peace Prize.

Roosevelt decided not to run for reelection in 1908, but in 1912 he ran unsuccessfully for president again. He ran under the banner of his own Progressive (Bull Moose) Party.

SITTING BULL
1834?–1890
Sioux Indian Chief

Sitting Bull was born in South Dakota. As a child, he was called Hunkesni, a Sioux word for slow. He earned the name Sitting Bull after showing great courage in a fight against the Crow Indians. It was a name which his father chose for him.

Sitting Bull became a medicine man. A year before the battle of the Little Bighorn, he received a vision that the Indians would triumph over their enemies. He was the leading medicine man in the preparations for the battle which fell on June 25, 1876. Before the battle, he led a sun dance. He inspired the Indians to fight to kill, not just to show off their courage in battle, or else they would lose their lands to the white people. This unexpected, new fierce way of fighting helped lead to the total defeat of General Custer and his soldiers. After the battle, Sitting Bull and his followers were driven up into Canada. In 1881 Sitting Bull returned to the U.S. where he was held at Fort Randall in South Dakota for two years. He then lived on the Standing Rock Reservation, where in 1890, he helped to start the Ghost Dance. Fearing another Indian uprising, the government sent police to arrest Sitting Bull. Both he and his son were killed in the process.

STALIN, Joseph
1879–1953
Russian dictator (ruled 1929-53)

Stalin (meaning "man of steel") was the political nickname of Joseph Vissarionovich Djugashvili. He fought vigorously and ruthlessly in the 1917 Russian Revolution and the civil war that followed. In 1922 he was made General Secretary of the Communist Party, one of the highest political offices in the Soviet Union. In 1924, after Soviet leader Vladimir Lenin's death, Stalin was one of a group of leaders who took power. In 1929 he became the only party leader.

Soon after Stalin became dictator, he began rebuilding Soviet industry and agriculture. To make farming more efficient, he forced the peasants to join "collective farms." These were huge areas of land worked jointly by thousands of people. Many peasants objected, and Stalin sent in his troops to stop any resistance.

During World War Two, Stalin joined Britain and the United States in a military alliance (partnership) against Germany. The bravery of

Joseph Stalin was dictator of the Union of Soviet Socialist Republics and led Russia to victory in World War Two. While he was in power, people lived in fear of his secret police.

Soviet soldiers on the eastern front, where millions died, helped to win the war. Almost as soon as victory was declared, Stalin ended his alliance with the West. The Soviets had freed several eastern European countries (including Poland, Czechoslovakia, and Hungary) from Nazi rule. Now Stalin joined them together as a "Soviet bloc."

In the late 1940s and early 1950s, Stalin made tough plans to rebuild national wealth. Once again he eliminated all opposition, sending those who disagreed with him to forced-labor camps or to exile (forced relocation) in Siberia.

Stalin died in 1953.

SUN YAT-SEN
1866–1925
Chinese leader

Sun Yat-sen was educated in Hawaii and became a doctor. When he was a student, he became eager for revolution in China, which was ruled at that time by the corrupt empress Tz'u Hsi. He began making speeches and writing articles encouraging rebellion, and Tz'u Hsi sent assassins to hunt him down. Sun Yat-sen escaped to England and later went to Switzerland.

While Sun Yat-sen was abroad, he continued to encourage revolution. He proposed that China should be a republic governed by three principles: nationalism (freedom from foreign interference), democracy (rule by elected politicians), and socialism (the creation of a welfare state to benefit all citizens).

In 1912, the revolution succeeded. The last Manchu emperor, a child, was removed from power. Democracy was declared. Sun Yat-sen was invited to be the Chinese republic's first president. But he was opposed by the powerful general Yuan Shikai and resigned after just six and a half weeks as president. Sun Yat-sen was forced to stay away from his country during another 11 years of civil war. It was not until 1923 that peace came again and Sun Yat-sen returned. Right up to the day he died, he never stopped fighting for a unified China.

Sun Yat-sen resigned as President of the Chinese government after six and a half weeks.

TECUMSEH
1765?–1813
Shawnee Indian leader

Tecumseh was born in Ohio, the son of a Shawnee chief. His name means "Shooting Star" or "Meteor." He and his brother, Tenskwatawa, known as the "Shawnee Prophet," worked to unite the Indian nations to resist the white settlers who were taking over the Indians' land.

Tecumseh and Tenskwatawa traveled great distances trying to persuade all the Indians to fight for their land against the white invaders. In 1811, Tecumseh went on a trip to convince more people to join him. The Indian Territory governor, William

Tecumseh, a Shawnee Indian leader who spent his life persuading Indian tribes to unite to defend their lands.

Henry Harrison, led the white settlers against the Indians during this time. At the Battle of Tippecanoe in November 1811, Tenskwatawa was killed, and the Indians lost many supplies.

Tecumseh then fought on the side of the British in the War of 1812, hoping to defeat the Americans. He was killed in battle while commanding his Indian forces in Canada.

THATCHER, Margaret
1925–
British leader

Although educated to be a chemist, Margaret Thatcher always had a keen interest in politics. She was elected to the British Parliament in 1959 and earned a reputation as a strong speaker and hard worker. From 1970 to 1974 she served as secretary of state for education and science.

In 1979, Thatcher became the prime minister of Great Britain, the first woman to hold this position. She was reelected twice, in 1983 and 1987. She resigned in 1990.

No other British prime minister in the twentieth century has held the position longer than she has.

Margaret Thatcher was the first woman ever to be elected Prime Minister of Great Britain.

WASHINGTON, George
1732–99
1st U.S. president (in office 1789-97)

Washington's father, a rich Virginia farmer, died when the boy was 11, leaving him to be brought up by his half-brother, Lawrence. Washington educated himself from the books in his brother's library, and also learned farming, hunting, riding, and other skills. When his brother died in 1752, he ran the family estates.

In 1759 Washington married a rich widow, Martha Custis. By this time Washington had had military experience, leading British soldiers against the French. He was also a politician and represented his fellow landowners in the House of Burgesses, the Virginia state legislature.

For the first 40 years of Washington's life, America was governed by Britain. Many Americans resented being ruled and taxed from the other side of the Atlantic Ocean. In 1775, discontent against the British flared into rebellion. After the Revolutionary War began, Washington was made commander-in-chief of the American forces. He performed brilliantly. Although the British army was bigger and far better trained, Washington's army held their own until France came to help the Americans in 1778. He finally defeated the British and forced them to surrender at Yorktown, Virginia in 1781. There was minor fighting for another few months but the Revolutionary War was over and the Americans had won.

After the war Washington led the Constitutional Convention. The people sent to it discussed how the new country was to be governed and who was to do it. In 1789, having decided on a republic rather than a monarchy (rule by a king or queen), the convention unanimously elected Washington president. He served for eight years and then retired from politics to run his estates. When he died two years later, he left a will freeing all his slaves.

George Washington crosses the Delaware River during the Revolutionary War. He was a great leader, and the first President of the United States of America.

PEOPLE OF ACTION

ADDAMS, Jane
1860–1935
U.S. social reformer

Addams was born in Cedarville, Illinois, to wealthy parents. She was horrified when she realized how the poor lived. In 1889, with her friend Ellen Starr, Addams bought Hull House in a poverty-stricken area of Chicago. At first, it was run as a private charity, providing leisure and medical facilities, a nursery, and classes in the arts and physical fitness. But Addams decided that poverty needed tackling at the state level. Armed with statistics, she successfully fought for laws to help and protect the poor. These laws insisted on safe conditions in factories, provided the first juvenile court, gave recognition to trade unions, and set an eight-hour day as the most a woman could work in a factory.

Gradually, Addams moved into national politics. She worked for women's right to vote and racial equality, and she spoke out against the United States's involvement in World War One. She was awarded the Nobel Peace Prize in 1931.

ANTHONY, Susan Brownell
1820–1906
U.S. reformer and women's rights leader

Anthony's father was a pioneer campaigner for the abolition of slavery. If women had been allowed to, she might have gone into politics as well. Instead, Anthony turned to public speaking and campaigning to persuade people to demand reforms.

She began by speaking against the use of alcohol. Her research into alcohol addiction took her to the slave plantations of the South, and she soon joined the campaign to abolish slavery.

In the 1850s, after making friends with Elizabeth Cady Stanton, Anthony took up a third cause: women's rights. For 50 years she fought to give women the right to vote and win for them equality in education, work, and marriage. She and Stanton founded a group that eventually became the National American Woman Suffrage Association. Anthony was president of this group from 1892 to 1900. She died before American women actually got the vote in 1920, but her tireless work had helped in the struggle to give women this important right.

ARMSTRONG, Neil
1930-
U.S. astronaut

As a young boy in Ohio, Armstrong learned how to fly airplanes and had his pilot's license when he was 16. He flew for the U.S. Navy during the Korean War and came back to school at Purdue University. He became an astronaut for NASA in 1962. On July 20, 1969, as commander of the spacecraft *Apollo 11*, Armstrong became the first human to set foot on the surface of the moon. His words as he stepped from the ladder of the landing craft *Eagle*, "That's one small step for [a] man, one giant leap for mankind," have become history. He left NASA in 1971 to teach. He received the Congressional Space Medal of Honor in 1978.

The first man on the moon: Neil Armstrong. The U.S. astronauts left on the moon the medals of the Russian cosmonaut, Yuri Gagarin, who died in 1968.

BARTON, Clara
1821–1912
U.S. educator and humanitarian

Clara Barton was born Clarissa Harlowe Barton in North Oxford, Massachusetts. She became a teacher, but illness forced her to give up teaching.

When the Civil War broke out in 1861, Barton became concerned about the needs of the soldiers. She wanted to help in some way. So she started nursing wounded soldiers in the Virginia area. Soon, she became known as the "Angel of the Battlefield." Barton did such a good job that she was named head of nurses for General Benjamin Butler's Union forces.

After the Civil War ended, Barton went to Europe to try to regain her own health. While in Geneva, Switzerland, she became interested in the work of the International Red Cross and volunteered to help civilians who had been injured in the Franco-Prussian War of 1870-71.

When she came back to the United States in 1873, Barton worked to form the American Red Cross. It was established in 1881. She was the first president of the American Red Cross and remained president until 1904, when she retired. Both Barton and her assistants gave help to countless victims of floods, hurricanes, fires, and other disasters.

Clara Barton was known as the "Angel of the Battlefield."

BLÉRIOT, Louis
1872-1936
French airplane pioneer

On July 25, 1909, Blériot was the first person to fly a plane across the English Channel, lying between France and England. He had burned his foot the day before and was on crutches. The morning of his flight was so misty that he had to ask bystanders in which direction lay the English Channel and Dover, his destination. His flight was the longest over water anyone had made up to that date. It lasted 37 minutes. Born in Cambrai, France, Blériot went on to found an airplane company that built many of the aircraft used by France in World War One.

BOLÍVAR, Simón
1783–1830
South American liberator

Bolívar was born in Caracas, Venezuela. As a young man, he went to Europe, where he was influenced by the ideas of Jean Jacques Rousseau and by the French Revolution. He vowed to free Venezuela from Spanish rule. When the Venezuelan revolution against Spain broke out in 1810, Bolívar joined a group of patriots. They seized the city of Caracas and proclaimed Venezuela's independence, but in 1812 the Spanish regained Caracas. Bolívar recaptured the city in 1813, but once again the Spanish overpowered him and his patriots (1815). Bolívar was forced into exile in Haiti. From there he led an invasion of Venezuela in 1816, where he captured the city of Angostura (now Ciudad Bolívar).

In 1819, Bolívar led his patriot army across the freezing, snow-covered Andes Mountains into Colombia. They took the Spanish there completely by surprise and defeated them at Boyacá, making Colombia independent. The new republic of Gran Colombia was proclaimed, and Bolívar was made its president. The republic included what are now Colombia and Venezuela. (Panama joined it in 1821 and Ecuador in 1822.) Bolívar returned to Caracas in 1821 and liberated Venezuela. Ecuador was taken from the Spanish in 1822. Bolívar next turned to Peru. He met with the Argentine liberator José de San Martín at Guayaquil. San Martín agreed to allow Bolívar and his army to be the liberators of Peru. The next year part of Peru was renamed Bolivia in Bolívar's honor.

Then Bolívar's dream of a united Spanish America began to come apart. The countries of Gran Colombia wanted more independence for themselves. Revolts broke out. In 1828, Bolívar tried to save Gran Colombia by declaring himself dictator. But the very next night he barely managed to escape an assassination attempt. The collapse of his republic continued. Venezuela and Ecuador seceded. In 1830, ill, tired, and discouraged, Bolívar resigned as president of Gran Colombia. Soon after that he died, poor and bitterly disappointed. But today Bolívar is regarded as one of South America's greatest heroes.

BOONE, Daniel
1734–1820
U.S. frontiersman

In Boone's boyhood, the settlers knew little about the interior of the American continent. Most settlements were made on the eastern coast. Only a few fearless adventurers crossed mountain ranges such as the Appalachians. These people were called "frontiersmen." Boone was one of the first and most colorful of them all. From 1769, he lived in the interior in the forest, and became famous for his hunting, trapping, tracking, and survival skills. He was captured by Indians in 1778 and was adopted by a Shawnee chief as a member of their nation.

In 1784, an account of Boone's adventures was published that made him a national hero, inspiring a legend of the hard-living, hard-fighting frontiersman. Boone continued exploring, usually alone, until he was over 70.

BOWIE, Jim
1796?–1836
U.S. frontiersman

Jim Bowie was a hero of the Texas Revolution, in which the early settlers of Texas fought for independence from Mexico. He may also have invented the bowie knife, a long-handled knife about 15 inches (38 centimeters) long. It was used by frontiersmen for hunting and fighting.

It is difficult to separate truth from legend in Bowie's life story. Some scholars think he was born in Logan County, Kentucky, and his family moved to Missouri and then Louisiana when he was a boy. After an adventurous early career, he went to Texas in 1828. Texas was then part of Mexico. Bowie became a Mexican citizen and married the daughter of a Mexican official.

Jim Bowie was a frontier hero who may have been the inventor of the bowie hunting knife.

As trouble between the Americans and Mexicans grew in Texas, Bowie took the side of the Americans. In 1835, he became a colonel in the army of Texas. Along with Davy Crockett and some 180 other Texans, Jim Bowie died in the fierce battle they fought against the Mexican army at the Alamo in San Antonio, Texas.

BYRD, Richard Evelyn
1888–1957
U.S. explorer and aviator

Byrd was born in Winchester, Virginia, and attended the United States Naval Academy. He learned to fly when he entered U.S. naval aviation. Byrd was put in charge of the fueling station for seaplanes trying to make the first Atlantic Ocean crossing. He designed several navigation aids that helped them make the crossing in 1919.

Byrd later joined a small expedition to Greenland and decided to attempt the first flight over the North Pole. He succeeded in 1926. Three years later, he set out to be first to fly over the South Pole, too. Once more, he succeeded, although he had to throw out his emergency supplies to make the plane light enough to cross Antarctica's Queen Maud Mountains.

Byrd later survived an entire winter alone in Antarctica, but he was no longer interested in personal success. Instead, he turned his attention to scientific discovery and research on the continent of Antarctica.

CABOT, John (Giovanni Caboto)
1450?–1498?
Italian sailor
and
CABOT, Sebastian
1484?–1557
Italian sailor

John Cabot, a sailor from Genoa, was probably the first European since the Vikings to reach the mainland of North America. In 1497, King Henry the Seventh of England sent him "to sail to all parts, countries, and seas of the East, of the West, and of the North," and to find lands no Christian had ever visited before. After several months of sailing west, Cabot reached land and claimed it for England. The land was probably what is now Cape Breton Island, Nova Scotia, Canada. John Cabot went on a second westward expedition in 1498 and never returned.

The explorers John and Sebastian Cabot. A famous map made by Sebastian Cabot of his and his father's discoveries is kept in Paris.

Sebastian Cabot, born in Venice, was one of John's sons. He spent many years making maps and exploring the coasts of North America and South America for the kings of England and Spain. He followed the routes of earlier sailors, checking and correcting ancient maps and charts.

During an expedition to South America, Sebastian Cabot was looking for El Dorado, "the Golden." Supposedly, the streets of this legendary city were paved with gold. Cabot never found it. But he did explore a bay in southeastern South America that he named Rio de la Plata. It means "Silver River." The sight of Indians wearing silver as part of their native dress may have prompted Cabot to call it that.

Later, Cabot published a fanciful account of his and his father's voyages. It was full of stories about sea monsters, giants, and fabulous events. Afterward, Sebastian joined his brothers in founding the Muscovy Company, created especially to find a northeast passage to Asia.

CHAMPLAIN, Samuel de
1567?-1635
French explorer

Champlain began exploring the coast and interior of Canada in 1603. He was content with a simple life and learned the ways and languages of the Indians. He spent most of his time in the western prairies and the northern hills and plains of what is now French Canada. In 1608, he founded Quebec, the first European settlement north of Florida.

Champlain explored the St. Lawrence River and set up trading posts to buy furs and dried fish from the local people. He discovered an enormous lake, as big as an inland sea. It lies across the boundary between Canada and the American states of Vermont and New York. It is named after him: Lake Champlain.

In 1613, the French king made Champlain governor of New France, as Canada was then called. In 1629, during fighting between the English and French, he was taken prisoner and sent to England. He returned to Canada in 1633 and died there two years later. Samuel de Champlain remains one of the most honored men in Canadian history.

CODY, William Frederick (Buffalo Bill)
1846-1917
U.S. frontiersman and showman

Nicknamed Buffalo Bill, William Cody led a life of adventure in the American West when it was still a wild and largely unsettled land. He was a rider for the Pony Express, a scout for the Union Army during the Civil War, and an Indian fighter.

After the Civil War ended in 1865, Cody became a hunter, providing meat for railroad construction crews. During these years, he earned his nickname by killing large numbers of buffalo that roamed in huge herds on the Great Plains. Later in life, he spent many years touring the United States and Europe with his "Buffalo Bill's Wild West" show. It featured exhibitions of riding and shooting as well as staged battles with Indians.

Buffalo Bill Cody's Wild West Show toured the United States and Europe.

COLUMBUS, Christopher
1451–1506
Italian sailor

Columbus was christened Cristoforo Columbo; Columbus is the Latin form of his name. Born in Genoa, Italy, the son of a weaver, he ran away to sea when he was in his teens. A few years later he was shipwrecked on the coast of Portugal, changed his name to Cristobál Colón, and settled there.

Columbus believed that there was a way to reach the rich trading countries of the East by sailing west across the Atlantic Ocean. He spent many years trying to persuade various European kings and queens to pay for an expedition that would prove him right and make them rich. In the end, his efforts were rewarded. King Ferdinand and Queen Isabella of Spain agreed to finance a small expedition: three ships and 90 men.

The ships set sail on August 3, 1492. After a stop at Gomera, in the Canary Islands, for food and water, they continued under a fair wind across the Atlantic. Land was sighted on October 12, 1492. Columbus thought he had reached Asia and that he had succeeded in sailing around the world. In fact, he was probably on Watling Island in the Bahamas. Columbus and his men sailed on and landed on another island, which he named Hispaniola (meaning "little Spain"). The island is now shared by the countries of Haiti and the Dominican Republic.

Although Columbus had failed to find the western sea-route to India as he had promised, the king and queen were encouraged by his discoveries in the Caribbean. In 1493 they sent him on a second voyage of exploration. He visited the islands now

Columbus first glimpses the "New World."

called Cuba (which he thought to be a peninsula of Asia), Guadeloupe, and Jamaica. Early in 1496 he returned to Spain.

Columbus's third voyage, in 1498, led to the discovery of Trinidad and the South American mainland. On his fourth and final voyage, in 1502, his ships reached the coast of Honduras, then sailed along the shores of Nicaragua, Costa Rica, and the Isthmus of Panama. They brought back much gold and information about the New World, but by now Queen Isabella was dying and King Ferdinand had lost interest in Columbus and his discoveries. It was not until several years after his death, when full exploration of the New World began, that people at last realized that Columbus had discovered a new continent.

COOK, James
1728–79
English explorer

Cook was one of the first Englishmen to sail around the world and explore the Pacific Ocean. He went to sea when he was 18, and he volunteered to join the Royal Navy in 1755. In those days, experienced volunteers were rare and earned quick promotion. Cook spent much of his time charting the east Canadian coast and the St. Lawrence River. This provided valuable information to both trading vessels and warships. In 1768, the navy sent him with his ship *Endeavour* to the southern hemisphere on a scientific expedition. Cook and his crew visited and mapped most of the coasts and channels of New Zealand and eastern Australia.

In 1772, he was sent on a second journey. This time he was to find out the size of Antarctica by sailing around it and to investigate the "Great South Land" further. During the winter, when the Antarctic Ocean was too ice-locked for exploration, Cook turned north into the Pacific Ocean. There, he charted Tahiti and the New Hebrides, and discovered New Caledonia.

In 1776, Cook made his final voyage. He had set out to find the Northwest Passage. This was supposed to be a sea route from the Atlantic to the Pacific that wound through the Arctic islands of northern Canada. He never found it. The voyage ended for him on February 14, 1779, when he was killed by some natives on the island of Hawaii during a fight there.

During his voyages, James Cook charted and claimed more land for Britain than almost any other explorer.

CORTÉS, Hernán (Hernando Cortez)
1485–1547
Spanish soldier

When Cortés was 19, he sailed to the New World, arriving on the island of Hispaniola in 1504. In 1511 he accompanied Diego Velázquez, the Spanish governor of San Domingo (Dominican Republic), on his expedition to Cuba. The Spanish were anxious to conquer the New World for two reasons; to spread the Christian faith and to take its wealth. Velázquez had heard of the riches of mainland America, especially the Aztec kingdom of Yucatan, where gold was supposed to be as common as wood or stone. In 1518 he suggested to Cortés that Cortés take command of an expedition to Mexico. Before permission was granted by Spain, Cortés took 600 Spaniards and a dozen horses and sailed for the mainland.

The Aztec people believed that one day their god Quetzalcoatl would come down to Earth to rule them. When they heard accounts of Cortés on horseback – the first white man and first horse ever seen in mainland America – they thought that he must be their god. Montezuma, the Aztec emperor, sent him gifts of gold, and Cortés pressed eagerly on, hoping to conquer the land where such riches could be found.

Cortés came at last to Tenochtitlan, capital of the Aztec Empire, where he was welcomed as a god. Cortés took Montezuma as his prisoner for six months and demanded ever-larger offerings of gold from the people. The Mexican people began to hate the Spanish invaders. Deciding to help them, Velázquez sent ships and soldiers to bring Cortés down. The conqueror defeated the forces and persuaded the men to mutiny against Velázquez and join him.

During Cortés' absence from Tenochtitlan, the Aztecs had besieged his followers in their city. Furious, Cortés led a Spanish army to recapture Tenochtitlan. After months of fighting, during which Montezuma was killed, the Aztecs finally surrendered. Cortés declared their empire Spanish, and the Spanish king made Cortés its governor. But the king had never forgiven Cortés for exploring without permission in the first place. He sent officers from Spain who gradually took over Cortés' power. In 1540 Cortés returned to Spain, where he died in poverty in 1547. Almost 20 years later his body was reburied in Mexico.

COUSTEAU, Jacques-Yves
1910–
French underwater explorer

In 1943, Cousteau and Emile Gagnan invented the aqualung, a portable, underwater breathing device. It greatly increased people's interest and capability in exploring the world's oceans. Born in St.-André-de-Cubzac, France, Cousteau wrote about exploration under the sea with an aqualung in *The Silent World* (1953). He also became a pioneer in underwater filming and research. Often he studied the underwater world in mini-submarines launched from his deep-sea exploration vessel *Calypso*. His films explaining the sea's mysteries and wonders became popular television programs.

guzmā. mıchvacā.

An Aztec drawing of Cortés (on horseback) conquering the people of Mexico.

Jacques Cousteau was a pioneer in underwater filming and research.

CROCKETT, Davy
(David Crockett)
1786–1836
U.S. frontiersman

Davy Crockett was a lawyer, but he earned a reputation as a tough-talking, hard-shooting frontiersman. He was elected to represent the southern state of Tennessee in Congress, serving three terms between 1827 and 1835. He then moved to Texas. During the Texas fight for independence from Mexico, Crockett was killed at the battle of the Alamo. His tough character and bravery are described in a song about him, which keeps his name alive today.

CUSTER, George Armstrong
1839–1876
U.S. Army officer

Custer attended the United States Military Academy at West Point. He graduated in 1861, at the bottom of his class. But he soon proved to be a very able soldier. The Civil War had just begun, and Custer fought bravely in many famous cavalry battles. Before the war was over, he had become the Union Army's youngest brigadier general, at only 23. Two years later, he was made a major general. After the war, Custer was dropped to the rank of captain, and when he was assigned to the Seventh Cavalry in 1866 it was as a lieutenant colonel. He commanded the regiment until his death.

In 1876, Custer and his men were assigned to assist in a campaign under General Alfred H. Terry against the Sioux and Cheyenne Indians. In June 1876 the U.S. forces reached what is now southern Montana. General Terry divided his troops into two groups. Custer's group was to approach the Indian encampment from the south, near the Little Bighorn River, and get into position to attack when Terry's forces arrived. On June 25, Custer's scouts found the Indian encampment. There were thousands of warriors in the camp, led by Crazy Horse, Gall, and Sitting Bull. But because many of the Indians were hidden in nearby ravines, Custer's scouts guessed that they numbered only about 1,000. Custer decided that his troops could easily defeat such a small group on their own without waiting for the rest of the U.S. force. He split his regiment into three groups. One, under Captain Frederick Benteen, was sent to keep the Indians from escaping to the south. Major Marcus Reno was sent across the river to attack.

Custer took about 200 men and headed north to charge into the Indian camp. The battle lasted less than an hour. Custer's group was quickly surrounded, and every man was killed. Benteen and Reno managed to lead what was left of their soldiers to safety in the hills to wait for Terry and the main U.S. force. The Indians broke camp and left the area.

The battle, which became known as "Custer's Last Stand," is still being argued about by historians and others.

Some believe Custer was wrong for not waiting to attack until Terry's forces had arrived. Some say Reno's men could have rescued Custer's group if they had remained in the battle. Others argue that General Terry should have known how many Indians were in the encampment.

What really happened will probably never be known.

DA GAMA, Vasco
1469?–1524
Portuguese explorer

Da Gama was the first European explorer to sail to India by traveling around the coast of Africa. At that time, India was an important center of the profitable spice trade. The Portuguese king wanted to control this trade, so in 1497 he sent Da Gama on a journey of exploration.

In 1479, Da Gama set off on his great voyage of exploration. He sailed from Portugal to India, rounding the Cape of Good Hope, off what is now South Africa, to do so. The parchment shown here chronicles his voyage. After he left Lisbon, he sailed to Saint Helena, rounded the Cape of Good Hope (Cupa de Boa Esperah), and on to Malindi before sailing across the Indian Ocean to Calicut.

With four ships and about 170 men, Da Gama set sail from Lisbon, Portugal, and bravely ventured west into the Atlantic Ocean. He then turned toward the African continent, sailed around its southern tip, and traveled up Africa's eastern coast. Da Gama reached what is now Kenya, where he hired an Arab navigator to guide his small fleet across the Indian Ocean.

Da Gama's ships landed at Calicut, India, in May 1498. Merchants there, however, did not like the idea of outsiders interfering in their spice trade. They refused to do business with Da Gama, who reluctantly returned home to Portugal. In 1502, he set out again for India with a bigger and better-armed fleet. En route, he founded a new Portuguese colony in Africa, called Mozambique. In India, Da Gama terrorized the spice merchants into making a trade agreement. After returning to Portugal in triumph this time, Da Gama retired from the sea.

Twenty years later, Da Gama made one more trip to India. He was sent as Portuguese viceroy ("king's representative") to settle a trading dispute in Calicut. It was his last voyage. He died soon afterward in India, and his body was taken home to Portugal for burial.

DOUGLASS, Frederick
1818–95
U.S. abolitionist

As an author, speaker, and editor, Douglass devoted his life to fighting slavery. Born a slave in Tuckahoe, Maryland, he was sent to Baltimore in 1826 to work for a new master. His new master's wife helped him to learn to read and write.

Douglass failed in his first escape attempt from slavery. Then, in 1838, he dressed as a sailor and left Baltimore on a ship. He went first to New York City and then to Massachusetts. Soon, he became active in the movement to end slavery – abolition.

When his autobiography was published in 1845, he was afraid that he would be arrested as a runaway slave. So he went to England. There, with the help of friends, he raised enough money to buy his freedom.

Returning to New York in 1847, Douglass started an antislavery newspaper, the *North Star*. He spoke out against job discrimination and segregated (separate) schools for blacks and whites. His home was part of the "underground railroad," a system of hiding places that helped runaway slaves reach freedom.

Frederick Douglass devoted his life to fighting slavery.

During the Civil War, Frederick Douglass recruited blacks for the Union Army. During the years that followed, he held several government posts, including U.S. minister to Haiti (1889-91).

DRAKE, Francis
1540?–96
English sailor

Sir Francis Drake was the first Englishman to sail around the world. He was born in Devonshire, England, and grew up among sailors in the shipyards. As a young seaman, he began attacking Spanish ships in the Gulf of Mexico for their rich cargoes. He also made raids on Spanish towns.

Drake was famous for his bold seamanship. He brought many treasures from his explorations back to Queen Elizabeth the First and was knighted by her.

This amounted to piracy. It was a crime for which he would have been hanged – had the Spanish been able to catch him.

In December 1577, Drake left on an expedition to travel from England to the southernmost tip of South America and then into the Pacific Ocean. No English ship had ever done this before. Drake succeeded and continued his journey up the coast of South America, raiding Spanish settlements along the way in Chile and Peru. He pressed on up the west coast of North America, traveling about as far as Vancouver Island in Canada. At this point, he turned away from the coast, sailed west across the vast Pacific Ocean, and continued around the world. No Englishman before him had ever done this. Drake returned to England in 1580 and was knighted by Queen Elizabeth the First for his achievement.

In the following years, a quarrel between the English queen and King Philip the Second of Spain grew very fierce. Elizabeth encouraged Drake to make daring raids against Spain, which finally led to war. In 1588, a huge fleet of warships known as the Spanish Armada sailed into the English Channel to attack England. Drake led the English fleet into battle and destroyed about half of the Spanish Armada. The remaining Spanish warships fled.

Drake then retired from the sea and went into politics. But his love of adventure never left him. In 1595, he set out again for the New World, but it was his last voyage. While sailing back to England the following year, Drake died and was buried at sea.

EARHART, Amelia
1897–1937?
U.S. aviator

In 1932, Earhart became the first woman to fly a plane solo across the Atlantic. In 1935, she made an even longer solo flight across the Pacific from Honolulu, Hawaii, to California. Two years later, while attempting to be the first person to fly all the way around the world, she vanished. No one has ever found out what happened to her or her plane.

ERICSON, Leif
died about 1025
Viking sailor and explorer

Ericson's father, Eric the Red, was the first Icelandic explorer to reach Greenland and had told his son about a fabulous country to the south and west of Greenland. This land had been seen from the sea by one earlier explorer but never visited. In about the year 1000, according to a tale called the "Saga of Eric the Red," Leif Ericson was returning from a voyage to Greenland. His ship was blown off course, and he found himself on the shore of a new land. Leif named it Vinland, after clusters of wild grapes he found growing. Many historians believe it was Newfoundland, Nova Scotia, or Massachusetts. That would mean that Leif was the first European to set foot in North America, nearly four centuries before Columbus. Others say that the whole story is fiction because it comes from a collection of adventure stories written by Leif's son nearly 50 years after the explorer's death.

FORD, Henry
1863–1947
U.S. businessman

When Ford was a young man, cars were built by teams of craftsmen, and only the very rich could afford to buy one. Ford dreamed of making cheap cars that anyone could afford. He made his first car in 1896 and founded the Ford Motor Company in 1903. To make cars cheaply he invented the "assembly line" now used in factories worldwide. On an assembly line, each person (or, today, perhaps a robot) does one job, over and over again. A product, such as a car, is moved very slowly along a conveyor belt. As it passes each worker a new part is added, or a new process takes place. At the end of the line the product is complete.

Ford's assembly line factories made hundreds of cars every day. By 1927, a million had been sold in the United States alone. Ford's best known car was the Model T, nicknamed "tin Lizzie." This is the kind of car used in the old Laurel and Hardy movies. When other manufacturers started making many different kinds of cars, Ford brought out a new model called the Model A.

Ford became very rich. He gave millions of dollars to charities, including the Ford Foundation, named for him.

Portrait of Henry Ford, engineer and founder of the Ford Motor Company.

HICKOK, James Butler (Wild Bill)
1837–76
U.S. frontier marshal

Wild Bill Hickok was known as a gunfighter and respected for his courage and skill. It is said he killed only in self-defense or in his job as a marshal, or sheriff.

Born in Troy Grove, Illinois, Hickok went to Kansas to drive a stagecoach. During this time, he got a reputation as a tough frontiersman. Armed only with a knife, he supposedly killed a bear that attacked him. Another time, he killed three gunfighters in a fight.

Hickok served as a scout for the Union Army in the Civil War. Afterward, he fought against the Indians and scouted for Lieutenant Colonel George Custer. As a U.S. marshal in several frontier towns, Hickok gained a reputation as a marksman against outlaws that quickly grew into legend.

In 1872, he joined Buffalo Bill in exhibitions of his sharpshooting skills throughout the East. But Hickok soon returned to the West. He was shot to death by Jack McCall in a saloon in Deadwood, a town in present-day South Dakota. After his death, Wild Bill Hickok's reputation as a fearless frontier hero grew even more.

James Butler Hickok had a reputation as a tough frontiersman.

HUDSON, Henry
?–1611
English explorer

Like many explorers, Henry Hudson tried to find the Northwest Passage, a northern sea route from the Atlantic to the Pacific. This route would allow trading ships to sail between Europe and Asia. Hudson failed, but he did explore and chart large areas of unknown territory in the frozen lands off the coasts of northern Norway, Greenland, and North America.

Virtually nothing is known of Hudson's early life. He was sent to explore North America by the Dutch East India Company. He explored Hudson

Henry Hudson was cast adrift in a small boat by his rebellious crew.

Bay, the Hudson Strait, and the Hudson River. They are all named after him, even though he was not the first European to explore them. In 1611, his crew rebelled against him and set him adrift in a small boat in the Hudson Bay. He was never seen again.

JONES, John Paul
1747–92
U.S. naval hero

Sometimes called the "Father of the American Navy," John Paul Jones was born John Paul in Scotland. In 1773, while he was captain of a merchant ship in the West Indies, his crew rebelled against him. In the fight on board, he killed one of the rebelling sailors in self-defense. Still, he was accused of murder, and so he fled to Philadelphia. To disguise his identity, he added "Jones" to his name.

John Paul Jones joined the Continental Navy and entered America's Revolutionary War. As captain of the *Bonhomme Richard*, he sailed in the North Sea. There, in 1779, he met the British ship *Serapis*, which was larger and better armed than Jones's ship. Their three-hour battle was one of the most memorable in U.S. naval history. His answer to the British demand to surrender – "Sir, I have not yet begun to fight" – became a famous slogan in the navy. The British ship finally surrendered. Two days later Jones boarded and sailed on in the

Serapis when the *Bonhomme Richard* sank.

From 1787 to 1789 John Paul Jones fought for the Russian Navy in a war with Turkey. Then he retired to France, where he died. He is buried at the U.S. Naval Academy in Annapolis, Maryland.

John Paul Jones is sometimes called the "Father of the American Navy."

KELLER, Helen Adams
1880–1968
U.S. writer and lecturer

When she was two years old in Tuscumbia, Alabama, Helen Keller had a serious disease that left her blind and deaf. The only contact she had with the outside world was by touch. She was so young, she had not learned to read or to speak properly.

But her parents refused to believe that this "wild creature" could not learn. They hired a dedicated teacher, Annie Sullivan, to train their daughter. She taught the child to communicate by using her hand to spell words into Helen's hand. Keller learned to "hear" by touching people's throats as they spoke and to talk by touching her own throat and experimenting until she made the same sounds. She was one of the first people to learn Braille. (This system, invented by Louis Braille, allows blind people to read by touching raised dots that represent letters.)

Thanks to Sullivan's hard work and her own enormous efforts, Keller was able to go to high school and was graduated in 1904 with honors from Radcliffe College. She spent her life lecturing and writing about her fight to overcome her disabilities and gave hope to thousands of handicapped people. She traveled to Europe and Asia as well as across America to raise money to help the blind. Keller never allowed people to treat her differently because of her disadvantages. This attitude made many people change the way they behaved toward all handicapped people.

KING, Martin Luther, Jr.
1929–68
U.S. civil rights leader

King grew up in Atlanta, Georgia, at a time when blacks and whites were treated very differently. Many whites felt that blacks were inferior and kept them apart or "segregated." Blacks had to live in separate areas from whites, and they had separate seats in public places. Some states denied blacks the right to vote. At 15, King entered Morehouse College in Atlanta, where he decided to become a minister.

When black people began to demand equal rights, King joined the struggle. He soon became a leader in this civil rights movement. King used Gandhi's methods of nonviolent protest, such as sit-ins and boycotts. He led marches and spoke at public meetings of his dream that one day all human beings would be treated equally. Even when white extremists bombed his house, he continued to preach nonviolence.

In 1955 and 1956 King successfully led the boycott against segregated buses in Montgomery, Alabama. He helped to organize the Southern Christian Leadership Conference to expand the nonviolent struggle against all discrimination. To protest black unemployment, King led the March on Washington on August 28, 1963. At this time he gave his famous speech, "I Have a Dream."

In 1968, speaking at a rally in Memphis, Tennessee, King was assassinated by James Earl Ray. His murder shocked the United States and the world. A few months later, Congress passed the Civil Rights Act of 1968, which helped lessen racial discrimination.

The third Monday in January is a legal holiday to honor King.

Martin Luther King was a black Baptist minister and civil rights leader who fought to gain equal rights for blacks. He was assassinated in 1968.

LEWIS, Meriwether
1774–1809
U.S. explorer
  and
CLARK, William
1770–1838
U.S. explorer

Lewis and Clark had quite a lot in common. Each had been born in a county of Virginia – Lewis in Albemarle, Clark in Caroline. Each had spent time in the U.S. Army. And each became governor of a U.S. territory – Lewis of the Louisiana Territory in 1807, Clark of the Missouri Territory in 1813.

But what these two are most famous for is the expedition they led in 1804. That year, U.S. President Thomas Jefferson sent Lewis and Clark to cross North America from east to west. They had several tasks. One was to find out if there was a sea passage between the Atlantic and Pacific Oceans. Another was to see if beavers and other fur-bearing animals lived in the west as well as in the east. And above all, they were to make contact with native Americans and to persuade them to accept being ruled by Jefferson.

Lewis and Clark traveled for months, moving inland along the Missouri River, making maps, and collecting rocks, animals, and plants. They visited many American Indians. The Mandans gave them guides, and the Shoshone gave them horses to help them on their way. After 18 months, they reached the Pacific coast in what is now the state of Oregon. They spent the winter there before returning and reporting to Jefferson.

The coast to coast expedition by Lewis and Clark across America did not lead to the discovery of a water route to the Pacific Ocean, but they gained valuable information on the land and native people and opened the way from east to west.

Lewis and Clark found no sea passage between the Atlantic and Pacific. But they did find a vast, beautiful land full of natural wonders. Their expedition helped open the way to the American West.

LINDBERGH, Charles Augustus
1902–74
U.S. air pioneer

Born in Detroit, Michigan, Lindbergh became the first person to fly solo across the Atlantic Ocean,

Charles Lindbergh flew alone across the Atlantic Ocean in an airplane called "The Spirit of St. Louis." He was the first person to do this.

nonstop from New York to Paris, in 1927. Several pilots had already been killed or injured while trying to set this historic record. His plane was named the Spirit of St. Louis. Later he wrote books about his trip. One of them won a Pulitzer Prize.

In 1932 his baby son was kidnapped and murdered. This led to a federal law on kidnapping.

Nelson Mandela and his wife, Winnie.

MAGELLAN, Ferdinand
1480?–1521
Portuguese explorer

Magellan (Fernão de Magalhães) sailed with the Portuguese navy to Morocco, India and the Far East. The Portuguese king refused to back him for a voyage of exploration, so he went to Spain where he offered his services to King Charles the First. Those who bought and sold rare spices could make a lot of money. At that time the Portuguese controlled the only sea route to the East Indies where the spices grew. Sailors had to sail east by way of the Cape of Good Hope, around Africa. Charles sent Magellan to find another route, to the west.

In 1519, Magellan sailed west with five ships across the Atlantic Ocean. They rounded the tip of South America by the dangerous seaway that is now called the Strait of Magellan. They reached a second vast ocean that Magellan named the "Pacific" because it seemed so calm after the stormy Atlantic. Three of the ships successfully crossed the Pacific and landed in the Philippines. Magellan was killed in a fight between two groups of Filipino natives. After buying spices, one of his ships, the *Victoria*, rounded the Cape of Good Hope and crossed the Atlantic to Spain. Magellan's work helped the first European expedition to sail all the way around the world.

MANDELA, Nelson Rolihlahla
1918–
South African civil rights leader

Mandela has become one of South Africa's most important leaders in the struggle for the rights of black people. After World War Two, the white government introduced the policy of apartheid ("separate development") in South Africa for blacks and whites.

Mandela was born in Umtata. In his youth, he met Mahatma Gandhi, who inspired him. Mandela became a lawyer, and in 1944 he joined the African National Congress (ANC), a political party working to win equality for blacks with whites in South Africa. He later became its president. For the next twenty years, he organized campaigns against the white South African government and its racist policies.

In 1962, Mandela was arrested, charged with sabotage and conspiracy, and sentenced to life imprisonment. The white authorities would not set him free or discuss black rights with him as long as he refused to order his followers to give up violence. He remained the ANC leader but had little contact with the outside world. Other leaders, notably his wife, Winnie Mandela, took up his struggle to win justice and equal rights for the black citizens of South Africa. There was an international campaign to secure his release from prison. Songs were written about him, and pop concerts arranged to draw attention to his cause. Nelson Mandela was finally released from prison in February 1990.

NIGHTINGALE, Florence
1820–1910
English nurse

Until Nightingale's time, there were few professional nurses. Most sick people were nursed by their own families, or by untrained men and women. These were little better than the jailers who "looked after" prisoners. Nightingale was determined to change this system and improve nursing standards. She trained as a nurse in Germany. In 1854 she took a team of 38 nurses to Russia to care for injured British soldiers in the Crimea. A war was raging there between Russia on one side and Turkey, France, Sardinia, and Britain on the other. Nightingale was known as "the lady with the lamp," because she went around with a lamp each night, making sure each man was as comfortable as possible.

In 1856, Nightingale returned to London. In 1860 she was given money to set up the first training school for nurses at St. Thomas's Hospital.

PEARY, Robert Edwin
1856–1920
U.S. explorer

Peary was a navy engineer who was interested in polar exploration. He made his first trip to the interior of Greenland in 1886, and led several more expeditions there between 1891 and 1897. He published his results in 1898 in *Northward Over the Great Ice.*

In 1909, after two failed attempts, Peary, his assistant Matthew Henson, and four Eskimos became the first explorers to reach the North Pole.

Even then, the story was not over. Another U.S. explorer, Frederick Alfred Cook, said that he had reached the pole months before Peary and that he had arrived home first. For months his story was believed. But then Peary produced photographs and other evidence. Cook had no proof. Everyone then accepted Peary's claim. In 1911 Congress recognized Peary's feat by making him a rear admiral. Cook later went to jail for taking money given to support his expedition.

PENN, William
1644–1718
U.S. colonial leader

The son of an English admiral, Penn had the chance of a glittering public career. But, as a Quaker, he believed that people should be free to worship God in any way they liked. He wrote books and pamphlets about Quakerism, which authorities thought were attacks on the Church of England. Government officials grew more and more angry with Penn. They even sentenced him to a year's imprisonment in the Tower of London.

Penn was freed with the help of a friend of his father – the Duke of York (later King James the Second). But Penn and his beliefs were still unpopular in England, and in 1682 he arrived in America to start a Quaker community. Penn and his followers were given a large piece of land west of the Delaware River. King Charles the Second had named the place Pennsylvania, Latin for "Penn's Wood." Here Penn set up a Quaker community, amazing the Indians by treating them as friends instead of attacking them. Gradually, the settlement grew, as Quakers and others moved from Europe to live there. Soon there was a thriving town. Penn called it Philadelphia, the city of "brotherly love."

William Penn insisted on tolerance of all religions that did not conflict with Christian beliefs.

PIZARRO, Francisco
about 1478–1541
Spanish adventurer

Pizarro was a Spanish army officer. While based in Panama, he went on Balboa's expedition across the Isthmus of Panama. Pizarro was one of the first Europeans to see the Pacific. Later, Spanish officials sent him to South America in search of a fabulously wealthy country they had heard of. This was the empire of the Incas (part of what is now Peru), ruled by the god-king Atahualpa. Pizarro and his men captured and executed Atahualpa. Once Pizarro had killed their god, the Incas fell defeated. They surrendered, and the Spaniards ruled Peru. For a time Pizarro was its governor. But he quarrelled with a fellow-officer. Both of them claimed the town of Cusco and the right to take its treasures. Pizarro executed the other officer. For this, the man's son had Pizarro killed.

POLO, Marco
about 1254–1324
Italian traveler and merchant

Polo's father and uncle, both merchants, went on a 14-year-long trading trip, traveling overland from Venice to China. Kublai Khan, Emperor of China, asked them to bring "one hundred learned men" to teach western wisdom to the Chinese people. But the only Westerner the Polos could find who was willing to go was Marco. He worked for Kublai Khan for 17 years as a trading and political ambassador. He traveled all over China, and even into Tibet and Burma. In 1292 Kublai Khan sent Polo back to Europe, as escort to a princess who was to marry the Persian emperor. The journey lasted three years and took Polo to Sumatra, India, Persia, and Turkey.

When Polo reached Venice at last, he planned to settle down. But during a war between Venice and a rival city, Genoa, Polo was taken prisoner. During the year he spent in jail, he dictated the story of his adventures to a fellow prisoner. It became a best seller. Polo was the first European to tell of the peoples and customs of the east. Some of the wonders he described – coal fires, printing presses, and paper money – must have sounded just as fantastic to readers of the time as tales of giants and monsters.

RALEIGH, Walter
1552?–1618
English adventurer

One of the most interesting and adventurous people in English history is Sir Walter Raleigh. He was a sailor, an explorer, a writer, a scientist, and even a pirate.

As a young man, Raleigh served in the army in Ireland and soon won favor with the queen of England, Elizabeth the First. She made him a knight, gave him a large estate in Ireland, and granted him permission to trade and colonize in the New World. He sent settlers to what is now the southeastern United States, but none of the settlements succeeded. Raleigh then returned to Ireland. There, he helped to bring about the use of tobacco and brought the potato from the New World.

Raleigh eventually lost the favor of the queen by secretly marrying one of her ladies-in-waiting. Hoping to regain his position with the queen, Raleigh embarked on a new expedition in search of El Dorado, a mythical land of gold in South America. The expedition failed.

The first English settlers were brought to North America by Sir Walter Raleigh. He also brought the first potatoes to Ireland. But Raleigh's career ended sadly when he received the death penalty from the King.

In 1603 the queen died. The new king, James the First, did not like or trust Raleigh. After leaving Raleigh in prison in the Tower of London for 12 years, he released him to lead another South American expedition. However, against the king's orders Raleigh attacked Spain. When he returned to England he was beheaded for disobeying the king. The public who saw Raleigh as a hero turned against the king.

REVERE, Paul
1735–1818
U.S. patriot

Revere learned the trade of silversmith from his father, and produced many famous works, including the seal of the state of Massachusetts. He was one of the heroes of the Revolutionary War. In 1773 he was one of the Boston citizens who dumped tea into the city's harbor in protest against the British tax on imported tea. The event became known as the Boston Tea Party and was one of the incidents that led up to the Revolutionary War.

Revere belonged to a secret society, formed to spy on the British troops. In 1775 he made his famous ride on horseback to Lexington to warn the colonists that the British were coming to attack. The Americans were waiting and defeated the British at the Battles of Lexington and Concord.

Paul Revere was one of the first heroes of the Revolution. He took part in the Boston Tea Party, and his famous nighttime ride on horseback alerted many patriots to the advancing British soldiers.

Revere continued in his trade and made many beautiful objects in silver and bronze. He also designed and printed the first banknotes to be used in the new American republic.

SACAJAWEA
1787?–1812?
Shoshone Indian guide and interpreter

Sacajawea was a Shoshone Indian born in Idaho. Her name means "Bird Woman." As a young girl, she was captured by enemy Indians and sold as a slave to a French-Canadian trapper named Toussaint Charbonneau. In 1805, the Lewis and Clark expedition started up the Missouri River during its exploration of the lands of the Louisiana Purchase. Sacajawea and Charbonneau joined the explorers as guides and interpreters.

Sacajawea had relatives among the Shoshone Indians along the expedition's route, and they helped the travelers by providing food and horses. She also made friends among other Indian tribes, who showed the way across the Great Divide, over the Rockies, and down the Columbia River to the Pacific Ocean. Sacajawea then guided the explorers along the return route.

Sacajawea helped guide the explorers Lewis and Clark on their famous expedition across the United States.

Monuments to Sacajawea can be seen in Montana, Oregon, Idaho, and North Dakota. A grave said to be hers is marked by a monument in the Wind River Reservation in Fort Washaki, Wyoming.

SULLIVAN, Anne
1866–1936
U.S. teacher

Anne Sullivan is remembered as the teacher of the blind and deaf author and lecturer Helen Keller. Born in Feeding Hills, Massachusetts, Sullivan became nearly blind from a childhood infection. At the Perkins Institution for the Blind in Boston, she learned the touch alphabet. With it, words are spelled out into the palm of a blind person's hand. She later regained her eyesight through a series of eye operations.

Anne Sullivan was sent by the Perkins Institution for the Blind to teach the seven-year-old Helen Keller, who was both blind and deaf and had never learned to speak. Sullivan taught Helen the touch alphabet. She also taught her Braille, a system of raised letters that blind persons can "read" through touch. She accompanied Helen to classes at the Perkins Institution for the Blind and later at Radcliffe College. There, she helped Helen with her classwork by using the touch alphabet. After Helen was graduated with honors, Sullivan went with her on lecture tours.

In the early 1930s, Anne Sullivan's eyesight began to fail again. By 1935, she was nearly blind. She died a year later.

Anne Sullivan is best known as the teacher of the blind, deaf, and mute child, Helen Keller.

TUBMAN, Harriet
1820?–1913
U.S. campaigner against slavery

Tubman was born into slavery in Maryland, but in 1849 escaped to Philadelphia. She soon began her dangerous work of smuggling black slaves to freedom. In 1857, she rescued her parents from slavery. A network system developed that was nicknamed "the underground railroad." People like Tubman were known as "conductors." She was wanted, dead or alive, in many slave-owning states but was so skilled at disguises that she was never caught. She led over 300 slaves to freedom. She helped so many to escape to freedom that she became known as "the Moses of her people." During the Civil War she worked as a cook and nurse for the northern army, and on one raid, she guided soldiers so that they could free over 700 slaves. After the war, she worked to provide schools for freed slaves and campaigned for women's rights. She traveled and lectured until she was well over 80.

SCIENTISTS

ARCHIMEDES
about 287–212 BC
Greek scientist and inventor

Archimedes lived in Syracuse in Sicily. He was famous as a mathematics teacher and inventor. He was particularly interested in what scientists now call mechanics: the study of how things move. He invented the "Archimedean screw," a way of raising water from one level to another by turning a large screw inside a hollow tube. It was originally used for bailing water from ships, but is more often used in irrigation and drainage machines.

Archimedes's best-known discovery is called "Archimedes's principle." It says that if an object is put into a fluid (a liquid or gas), it appears to lose an amount of weight equal to the weight of fluid displaced. He is said to have worked this out in the bathtub, while wondering how to find out if the gold in the king's crown was pure or mixed with cheaper, lighter metals. He realized that if the crown was pure gold, it would displace the same amount of water as a lump of gold that weighed the same. If it contained a mixture of lighter metals, it would displace more water. He was so excited about his discovery that he leaped out of the bath, shouting "Eureka" ("I've found it"), and ran off to tell the king.

When the Romans invaded Syracuse in 212 BC, Archimedes helped his city by inventing defense machines such as boulder-hurling catapults and even, it is said, by setting fire to the sails of the

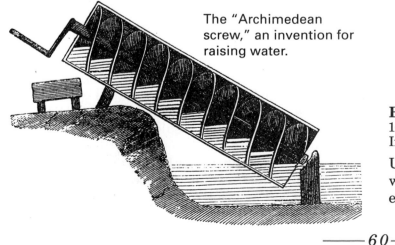

The "Archimedean screw," an invention for raising water.

Roman ships by focusing the sun's rays through a series of mirrors. In spite of this, the Romans captured the city. A Roman soldier saw Archimedes drawing diagrams in the sand of the marketplace, trying to work out what had gone wrong. Thinking that the circles and triangles he saw were battle plans, the soldier took Archimedes for a spy and killed him.

BANTING, Frederick Grant
1891–1941
Canadian scientist

Banting was part of a team of scientists who discovered insulin, the hormone that controls the amount of sugar in the blood stream. This discovery led to the treatment of diabetes. Without a daily dose of insulin, diabetics (people unable to control their own blood-sugar levels) would die.

Banting received the 1923 Nobel Prize for medicine for this discovery. He was born in Ontario and served in the Canadian Army during both world wars.

Canadian scientist Frederick Grant Banting won a Nobel Prize for his work on insulin.

BOYLE, Robert
1627–91
Irish scientist

Until Boyle's time, most scientists still agreed with medieval alchemists that everything in existence was made up of four elements: earth, air, fire, and water. Boyle's book, *The Sceptical Chemist*, changed all that. He showed that matter consists of compounds and mixtures made of many dozens of elements (over 100 are now known). If the balance of the elements in a mixture or compound is changed, a different substance is produced.

Boyle also researched sound waves and air pressure. He is remembered today for "Boyle's Law," which says that at constant temperature the volume of a gas decreases as the amount of pressure increases.

BURBANK, Luther
1849–1926
U.S. scientist

Burbank was a horticulturist, an expert in preparing and using land to grow fruits, vegetables, flowers, and other plants. He was born in Lancaster, Massachusetts, but made his reputation in California. Burbank used scientific methods to breed plants that would produce better crops, be more tolerant of bad weather, and have greater resistance to disease. His greatest successes were with potatoes, tomatoes, and such soft fruits as strawberries, plums, and peaches. He developed the nectarine, a variety of smooth-skinned peach. He also developed the white blackberry and the Shasta daisy. The town of Burbank, north of Los Angeles, is named after him.

CARVER, George Washington
1864–1943
U.S. agricultural chemist and researcher

Carver became known worldwide for his agricultural research and for his efforts to help farmers in the South. Born a slave, he was orphaned soon after his birth. He was raised by Moses and Susan Carver, who had been his owners until slavery was abolished in 1865. They taught him to read and write, and later he attended a school for black children. He earned both a bachelor's and master's degree at college, and in 1896 he became head of the agricultural department at Tuskegee Institute (now Tuskegee University), a black agricultural school in Alabama. His work on soil conservation and other ways to improve crop production was very important. Farmers in the South had been raising mostly cotton, which had worn out the soil. Carver told farmers about other crops they could raise and how these crops could be used. He developed many products from sweet potatoes, soy-

beans, and cotton waste. He also found more than 300 different uses for peanuts. He received many prizes and awards for his work. He lectured about the uses of peanuts all around the United States. He even spoke to Congress about peanuts in 1921.

Improving relations between black and white people was another of Carver's interests. He worked to help the races get along better with each other.

Three years before Carver died, he gave his entire life savings of $33,000 to Tuskegee Institute to establish a foundation for agricultural research. After his death, the farm where he was born became a national monument.

CAVENDISH, Henry
1731–1810
English scientist

Cavendish was the youngest son of a well-to-do family. He inherited a fortune, which he spent on scientific research of electricity, chemistry, and heat.

He also did research into gases. By treating metal with acids, he succeeded in identifying the element hydrogen. He also proved that water is made up of hydrogen and oxygen. Cavendish experimented with the effects of electric sparks on gases.

Born in Nice, France, Cavendish lived in London. He gave money for scientific research, especially to Cambridge University, which named the Cavendish Laboratory after him. It later became one of the most famous research laboratories in the world.

Henry Cavendish was able to devote his life to scientific investigations, thanks to a fortune he inherited from his uncle.

COPERNICUS, Nicolaus
1473–1543
Polish astronomer

Some people before Copernicus had believed that the sun and not the Earth was the center of the solar system. Aristarchus, for one, suggested it in the third century BC. But Copernicus was the first person to support it scientifically, by the exact observation of star movements in the sky.

Copernicus was a Roman Catholic priest. He knew that his book *On the Revolutions of the Heavenly Spheres* would cause a scandal, because it went against the Church's teaching that God created the Earth as the center of the universe. He therefore refused to publish the book until very late in his lifetime. When it did come out, soon after his death, it caused a sensation. Astronomers realized that it disproved the Earth-centered ideas of Ptolemy, which had stood almost unchallenged for 1,400 years. Led by Galileo and Kepler, they set about making accurate observations and exact calculations to prove that Copernicus was right.

CURIE, Marie
1867–1934
Polish-born French scientist
CURIE, Pierre
1859–1906
French scientist

Marie Curie studied science at Sorbonne University in Paris. There, she married a young science professor, Pierre Curie, and together they worked to investigate the rays given off by substances such as thorium and uranium.

As a result of their experiments, the Curies discovered an important substance, which they called radium. It was very difficult to purify. To produce just one gram of radium required tons of a radioactive ore called pitchblende.

The Curies thought their discoveries so important for the human race that they refused to patent their process or to make money from it. Instead, they published the information openly for all to use.

In 1906, three years after he and Marie won a Nobel Prize for their discovery, Pierre Curie was killed in an accident. In 1909, Marie Curie became professor in his place, and in 1911 she won a second Nobel Prize for her research with radium and polonium. She devoted the rest of her life to exploring the properties of radioactive substances, becoming head of an important laboratory in Paris that had been created for her. Her death from leukemia was probably caused by exposure to large amounts of radiation over her lifetime.

DARWIN, Charles Robert
1809–82
English scientist

As a boy, Darwin thought of going into the Church. He studied theology at Cambridge University. But his other passionate interest was botany, and he spent many hours studying plants. When Darwin left the university, he decided to take a few years off before finally deciding his future and got a job as official naturalist on the British ship *Beagle*. The *Beagle* was to spend five years exploring the world's southern oceans, making scientific observations.

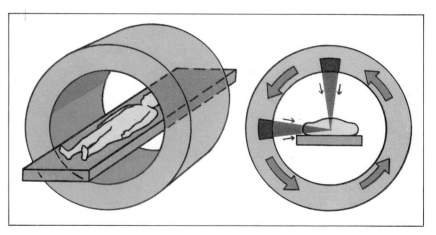

Marie Curie was born in Poland but lived in France. With her husband, she discovered radium. The use of X rays in hospitals developed from this discovery, and had it not been for the Curies, life-saving body scanning machines (right) would not have been possible.

When Charles Darwin first wrote about his theories of "natural selection" and human evolution, he was criticized by many religious leaders and writers. Today, although not everyone agrees with them, his ideas are accepted by most scientists studying life on earth.

The *Beagle* explored the coast of South America, the Galápagos Islands, Tahiti, New Zealand, and Tasmania. During this time, Darwin made notes about every plant and creature he saw and about how each was adapted to its environment.

When Darwin returned to England in 1836, he married and began a quiet life of studying and writing. He published an account of his travels, *The Voyage of the Beagle*. He also wrote books and articles on scientific subjects. But all the time he was thinking out an entirely new theory about how the world and its creatures came to be the way they are.

In 1858 Darwin presented his ideas in public, and in 1859 he published a book *On the Origin of Species by Means of Natural Selection*. He suggested, as a few others had before him, that plants and animals have not stayed the same since the beginning of time. He called the reason for the changes "natural selection." Darwin thought that some members of a species (kind of plant or animal) had certain traits that helped them survive in nature. He believed they lived longer than members who did not share their favorable traits, and they passed these traits down to their children. In this way, the species as a whole could change and grow more successful.

The suggestion behind this theory caused an uproar. The religious authorities were very upset. Newspapers rushed to ridicule his ideas. But many distinguished scientists spoke up for him. Within ten years, Darwin's ideas were known and were an inspiration to scientists all around the world.

Darwin went on writing, adding evidence he believed would support his theory. In 1871, he published *The Descent of Man*, which suggested that the human race had evolved (or changed) over millions of years just like any other species. Once again religious leaders opposed him; once again scientists leaped to his support.

Darwin's theory is easy to understand. But in the nineteenth century it was news and caused much discussion and argument, which continues to this day.

EINSTEIN, Albert
1879–1955
German-born U.S. physicist

Einstein was born in Ulm, Germany. He went to school in Switzerland and later lived and worked there. He came to the United States in 1933 and became a U.S. citizen in 1940.

The idea that nothing is absolutely stationary is known as the "theory of relativity." It had been suggested in 1904, but it was Einstein who developed it and backed it up with mathematical proof.

Einstein made many important discoveries. He showed, for example, that the speed of light cannot be exceeded. He also stated — and later experiments proved him correct — that as the velocity of an object increases (that is, as it moves faster), its mass also increases, and that mass and energy are equivalent. This is expressed mathematically as $E = mc^2$.

So far, Einstein had produced what he called the "special theory of relativity," applied to motion that is constant and does not accelerate. He went on to consider accelerating systems in what he called the "general theory of relativity." His calculations showed that gravity and acceleration affect objects in exactly the same way.

Albert Einstein is known as one of the greatest thinkers of the twentieth century.

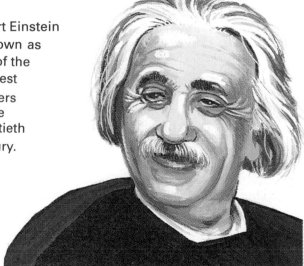

Einstein's ideas completely changed the way scientists thought. Until his time, they had always worked toward such things as exactness and absolute truth. Their explanations had depended on all human beings sharing the same viewpoint. That is, we observe time, space, and other phenomena in the same way. Einstein's theory meant that nothing was certain. If we look at time or space on another planet, or from outer space, they might be totally different from our earthly idea of them. For physics, this was a revolutionary idea.

FAHRENHEIT, Gabriel Daniel
1686–1736
German scientist

Fahrenheit invented a system of measuring temperature. The coldest temperature he could determine was 0°F (zero degrees Fahrenheit), the freezing point of water mixed with salt. He also determined that water alone freezes at 32°F. On the same scale, water boils at 212°F. Gabriel Fahrenheit was born in Danzig, which is now named Gdansk, in Poland.

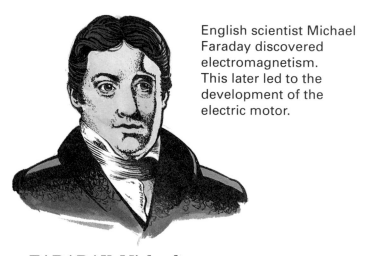

English scientist Michael Faraday discovered electromagnetism. This later led to the development of the electric motor.

FARADAY, Michael
1791–1867
English scientist

Faraday was born near London and became a bookbinder's apprentice. Determined to educate himself, he went to public lectures on chemistry at the Royal Institution in London. He impressed the lecturer, who gave him a job as a laboratory assistant. In 1825, Faraday was put in charge of the Royal Institution laboratory. Six years later, he was made a professor.

Faraday's first experiments were with gases. He discovered that gases could be turned to liquid by putting them under pressure. But his most important work was on electromagnetism. He found that a moving magnet produces a current in a coil. He also demonstrated that if two coils, insulated from each other, are wound on the same iron ring, a current flowing in one will cause a current to flow in the other. Faraday's work led to the development of the electric motor, the dynamo, and the transformer. The electrical unit of measurement called the *farad* is named in his honor.

FERMI, Enrico
1901–54
Italian-born U.S. scientist

Fermi worked on radioactivity. As a young professor at the University of Rome, he explained what happens during radioactive decay. It was another 22 years before anyone could prove that his theory was correct.

In 1934, Fermi discovered that some nonradioactive elements can be made radioactive. He also discovered that certain materials can slow down certain atomic particles, called *neutrons*, passing through them. This work won him the Nobel Prize for physics in 1938.

In the United States, Fermi went on with his experiments. He and his colleagues fired neutrons at uranium atoms and found that each atom split into two unequal pieces. This is called *nuclear fission*, or "splitting the atom." A chain reaction could be

Enrico Fermi delivering a lecture.

set up that would continuously cause uranium atoms to split apart. If the chain reaction could be controlled, it would provide energy. If the chain reaction could not be controlled, it would cause an enormous explosion.

During this time, World War Two was under way. President Roosevelt set up a top-secret team, including Fermi, to make a bomb using atomic fission. They code-named their experiments "the Manhattan Project," and in 1942 they developed the first atomic bomb.

FLEMING, Alexander
1881–1955
Scottish scientist

Fleming was a bacteriologist, researching ways of controlling the tiny organisms that cause infection. He grew bacteria for his experiments in a special kind of jelly smeared in glass laboratory dishes. One day he noticed that mold had grown on part of the jelly in one of the dishes, and that there were no bacteria anywhere near it. Something in the mold had killed them.

Fleming wrote about his discovery in 1929. But it was not until ten years later that he, together with Howard Florey and Ernst Chain, managed to separate the bacteria-killing substance from the mold. They made it into a drug that would prevent or cure infection. The drug is penicillin, and it is still one of the main drugs called antibiotics that save millions of lives each year.

The discovery of penicillin won Fleming, Florey, and Chain the Nobel Prize for medicine in 1945.

GALILEO
1564–1642
Italian scientist

Galileo is always known by his first name. His full name was Galileo Galilei, and he was born in Pisa. He came to believe that if an idea could be proved, it was real. If it could not be proved, it was not real. This view directly opposed religious teaching of the time.

Italian scientist Galileo dropping two objects from the leaning tower of Pisa.

As a young man Galileo studied medicine, mathematics, and physics at the University of Pisa. He was interested in the physics of motion. One day, after watching a lamp in Pisa cathedral and timing its swings with his pulse, he noticed that each swing took the same amount of time. Galileo discovered the law of the pendulum at the age of 20. On this basis, he invented the hydrostatic balance, an instrument used to find an object's specific gravity by weighing it in water.

At age 25, Galileo returned to the University of Pisa as a mathematics professor. There he discovered the law of falling bodies, which states that all objects fall to earth at the same speed, no matter what their size or weight.

Galileo's discovery caused an uproar. It challenged the teaching of the Greek philosopher Aristotle, who 2,000 years earlier had claimed that objects fall at different rates according to their weights. Galileo was forced to leave the University of Pisa and in 1592 he went to teach at the University of Padua, where he stayed for 18 years. At Padua, he investigated the expansion and contraction of metals. His work on mercury led him to invent the thermometer. Galileo also invented the sector, a type of compass still in use today.

Galileo heard of the recent invention of the telescope by Hans Lippershey. Beginning in 1609, Galileo built and sold his own telescopes throughout Europe. They were larger and more powerful than earlier models.

At first, astronomy was a hobby, but it soon came to occupy all of Galileo's time and led to his most important scientific work. He made several observations about the solar system now taken for granted. His study of the sky was always supported by thousands of hours of observation and page after page of mathematical proofs. It led him more and more to share Copernicus's view that the Earth moves around the sun and not the sun around the Earth. When he began teaching and writing about this theory, Church authorities ordered him to stop or risk punishment.

By this time Galileo was in his 50s, a frail, sick man. But he found it impossible to keep silent about things he thought were facts provable beyond doubt. When he was 68, he wrote a book comparing old and new views of the universe, and favoring the new. The Church authorities ordered him to state publicly that he was wrong, which he did.

Imprisoned in his villa in Florence, Galileo spent his last years writing a book summing up his life's work on force and motion. He became blind before the book was published and died five years later.

HIPPOCRATES
about 460–377 BC
Greek doctor

In ancient Greece, the practice of medicine often depended less on knowledge than on the supernatural: spells, potions, and magic ceremonies.

Hippocrates, the "father of medicine."

Hippocrates, a doctor on the island of Cos, began the change to a more modern style of medicine. He tried to study disease scientifically, working out its causes and listing its symptoms and its cures. He told his patients that their illnesses were caused not by gods or evil spirits but by natural causes. He said that they were more likely to be cured by proper treatment than by spells.

Hippocrates's fame quickly spread, and Cos became a healing center, with sick people flocking for cures and students hurrying to learn his methods. He published over 70 books, with such titles as *Epidemics, Epilepsy,* and *A Healthy Environment.*

Until recently, modern doctors used to take an oath based on the one Hippocrates taught his students: the "Hippocratic oath." It included such ideas as "I promise to help the sick to the best of my ability and judgment" and "I promise to avoid causing harm, and will not knowingly give or suggest harmful treatment."

HUBBLE, Edwin
1889–1953
U.S. astronomer

Hubble is best known for his studies of distant space. Working with the huge telescope at Mount Wilson Observatory in California, Hubble investigated the unproven idea that distant galaxies are moving away from us.

Hubble first decided to try finding out the speed of galaxy movement. He successfully did this by measuring changes in the light that galaxies gave off. The light changes he found are known as the red shift, and they proved that the galaxies are in fact moving. His research then led him to propose

what is now called Hubble's Law. This law says that the farther away a galaxy is from us, the faster it is moving away from us.

The Hubble Space Telescope, built to study distant space and launched in April 1990, was named for this pioneering scientist.

Johannes Kepler discovered the true pattern of the orbits of planets.

JENNER, Edward
1749–1823
English doctor

Jenner worked in the farming town of Berkeley in Gloucestershire, England, where he had been born. Jenner had heard local rumors that anyone who had cowpox (a mild sickness humans caught from working with cows) would be immune to smallpox, a far worse and often deadly disease. He wondered if he could prevent people from catching smallpox by first giving them a small dose of cowpox. To test the idea, he gave an eight-year-old boy a dose of cowpox, followed 48 days later by a dose of smallpox. The child survived. Jenner called this treatment *vaccination* after the Latin word *vacca*, meaning "cow." The method has been used to prevent all kinds of infectious diseases ever since.

Edward Jenner. There was violent opposition to the use of vaccination for a year after he first demonstrated it. It was only after seventy prominent physicians signed a declaration that they were totally confident in vaccination that it began to be commonly used by doctors.

KEPLER, Johannes
1571–1630
German astronomer

Kepler was a mathematician who discovered three laws of planetary motion. He was born in Weil, Germany. At the age of 25, he was made a professor of mathematics at Graz University in Austria. In 1600, Kepler left Graz to work with astronomer Tycho Brahe in Prague, which is in present-day Czechoslovakia. In 1601, he succeeded Brahe as royal astronomer.

With the aid of Brahe's detailed observations, Kepler was able to formulate the laws of planetary motion. He showed that each planet moves around the sun not in a circle, as had been believed until then, but in an oval shape called an *ellipse*. He suggested that tides in the sea might be caused by the movement of the moon. This idea was later studied by Isaac Newton when he was working on the theory of gravitation (attraction between planets and other large objects in space). By using precise observations and exact calculations, Kepler was the first person to try to prove Copernicus's theory that the Earth is in motion. Kepler's work was important not only to astronomy but also to the development of mathematics that took place in the 1600s.

LAVOISIER, Antoine Laurent
1743–94
French scientist

Lavoisier was the founder of modern chemistry. After careful experiments, he gave the first scientific explanation of the mysteries of fire. For 15 years he was head of the Royal Gunpowder Administration Office, developing safer and more effective guns.

When the French Revolution came, Lavoisier worked for the revolutionaries. He helped to standardize the metric system, making centimeters, meters, and kilometers the rule all over France. But because of his years as a royal tax collector, the leaders of the French Revolution did not trust Lavoisier. He was put to death on the guillotine.

Antoine Lavoisier, one of the founders of modern chemistry.

LEAKEY, Louis Seymour Bazett
1903–72
English anthropologist

Leakey was interested in paleontology (the study of fossil bones). He worked in Kenya, and spent his vacations with his wife Mary and sons Jonathan and Richard unearthing the sites of prehistoric human settlements.

The Leakeys were looking for the oldest human bones they could find. Until then, most scientists believed that the human race had existed on Earth for little more than half a million years. They thought that human beings had been "civilized" for only about 10,000. The Leakeys, however, found skulls, footprints, and other remains that prove our ancestors lived in Africa around 3.7 million years ago. The Leakeys' best-known find was the skull of a being called *Homo habilis* ("skilful human"), because he or she was the first person known to have made and used tools.

LEEUWENHOEK, Anton Van
1632–1723
Dutch scientist

Leeuwenhoek is known for perfecting the microscope. He used it to study the human body in detail never seen before. He was the first person to see how blood flows through the capillaries (veins as thin as hairs) and to describe blood cells. He also prepared his own magnifying lenses. Leeuwenhoek is known as the "Father of Microbiology."

LINNAEUS, Carolus (Carl von Linné)
1707–78
Swedish scientist

Linnaeus invented the method of classifying and naming plants and animals, which is still used today. This is known as the "binomial" system (bi=two; nom=name) because the name of each species consists of two parts, given in Latin. The first part is the genus ("group"), such as *Canis* (dog) or *Felis* (cat). The second part is the particular type of animal or plant belonging to that genus. For example, the wolf is known as *Canis lupus*, and the European wildcat as *Felis sylvestris*.

Linnaeus himself named thousands of different plants, but his system has grown and changed over the years, now covering millions of animals and plants.

NEWTON, Isaac
1642–1727
English scientist

Newton spent a lonely childhood. His father was a prosperous farmer who died when Isaac was a baby. Isaac's mother remarried, so he was brought up by his grandmother. Ignored by the village children, who thought him a snob, Newton spent much of his childhood alone, reading books and making things.

The result was that when Newton went to Cambridge University at 19, he already knew more than many of his professors. In 1669 he was made Professor of Mathematics, a job he kept for the next 32 years.

Newton's first scientific work was the study of light, or "optics" as he called it. He bought a prism at a fair, and used it to show that "white" light, for example sunlight, can be split up into the seven colors of the rainbow. If you pass the colors through a second prism they recombine to form "white" light again. He called the range of colors the spectrum.

Newton also studied motion. About 150 years earlier, when Copernicus was wondering why planets orbit the sun, the only answer he could

Sir Isaac Newton is seen here focusing white light through a prism to break it up into a spectrum. He is surrounded by other things with which we associate him, such as the apple tree.

think of was "Because they do." Later, Galileo had shown that since all natural movement is in a straight line, a force is needed to keep the planets around the sun in a curved path. Newton suggested that this force was the same as that which makes a ripe apple drop from a tree to the ground. He said that bodies such as the Earth pull other objects towards them (making them "gravitate" or move). The bigger the body, the bigger the "gravitational force."

In 1687 Newton published a book, *Philosophiae Naturalis Principia Mathematica*. It developed his ideas on gravity and gave mathematical proofs. He showed that the laws of gravitation mean that the planets must orbit (go around) the sun in ellipses (flattened circles). This is because they move faster when they travel towards the sun (pulled by its gravity) and slower when they move away (held back by its gravity).

Newton also formulated three laws of motion.

The first says that objects need forces to move them, stop them, or change their speed or direction. No object moves of its own accord. The second says that if two objects are to move with the same acceleration, the greater mass needs greater force to move it. The third says that whenever force is applied to an object, the object exerts an equal and opposite force. These laws help explain many things about how and why things move, on Earth and in space. They have been slightly changed by Albert Einstein's theory of relativity, but remain Newton's most vital contribution to science.

To help make his calculations simpler, Newton developed a new way of calculating, which he called "fluxions." It was similar to Gottfried Leibniz's calculus of 1684. This led to a furious argument about which came first. Calculus, whether Newton's or Leibniz's, is one of the sources of modern math. It has been a vital tool of science ever since it was invented.

PASTEUR, Louis
1822–95
French biologist

The son of a tanner, Pasteur taught science at Dijon, Strasbourg, and Lille Universities and then in Paris. In his spare time he did research. In 1857 he began experiments to see why liquids such as milk ferment (turn sour). He discovered that fermentation is caused by microorganisms known as bacteria. If these bacteria are killed by heating the liquid, and are prevented from returning, then fermentation does not occur. This showed that bacteria do not simply come into existence, as had been thought until then, but breed like other living things. The process of sterilizing liquids – killing the bacteria in them by heating – became known as "pasteurization." It is still used all over the world.

Pasteur went on to wonder if diseases in other living things might be caused by bacteria. He researched first into silkworm disease and then into chicken cholera. He found that both are caused by bacteria. He decided to try Edward Jenner's idea of vaccination. This involves using a less dangerous substance to inoculate (build up a defense) against a more deadly one. Pasteur grew cholera bacteria in the laboratory and made from them a vaccine (substance for vaccination) that successfully slowed down or stopped the real disease. He went on to develop successful vaccines against anthrax and rabies. Improved versions of these vaccines are still used today.

Not everyone admired Pasteur. Some doctors (for example Sir Joseph Lister) welcomed his work. Others, however, resented anyone without a medical degree trying to cure disease. He annoyed hostesses at dinner parties by refusing to shake hands for fear of infection. And he wiped even the cleanest-looking knives and forks on his napkin before using them. But the newspapers loved him and carried what they called the "germ theory of disease" all around the world. The French people collected money to build the Pasteur Institute in Paris in his honor. It is now one of the world's main centers of research into microorganisms and disease.

PRIESTLEY, Joseph
1733–1804
English chemist

Until Priestley's time, most chemists believed that there was a gas called phlogiston in every substance. This gas was released when the substance was burned. But no one had ever actually found phlogiston, and Priestley helped to disprove its existence.

Joseph Priestley was the first scientist to produce pure oxygen.

Priestley studied to become a minister, but he was also interested in chemistry. In his best-known experiment, he heated mercury oxide in the laboratory and produced pure oxygen for the first time. He went on to study the new gas and showed that a candle could burn in it, plants could produce it, and a mouse could survive in it. He also studied other substances and was the first person to isolate ammonia, sulfur dioxide, and hydrogen chloride in the laboratory.

Louis Pasteur at work in his laboratory.

SALK, Jonas Edward
1914–
U.S. doctor and scientist

Dr. Salk studied viruses and developed a vaccine in 1953 that prevented people from getting a virus called polio (poliomyelitis). Polio was a very serious disease that often left people crippled. In order to be sure that the vaccine was safe, he tested it first on monkeys. Then, to find out if it would really keep people from getting polio, he gave it to himself, his family, and almost two million school-children. By 1955 he knew that the vaccine worked. Although a later vaccine could be taken by mouth, Dr. Salk's vaccine had to be injected by a needle.

Salk also studied the viruses that cause flu (influenza). In the late 1980s he worked to try to find a vaccine to keep people from getting AIDS, a very serious disease from which many people were dying. After 1964 he was director of the Salk Institute for Biological Studies in California.

Evangelista Torricelli was a student of Galileo.

TORRICELLI, Evangelista
1608–47
Italian scientist

Torricelli was a student of the great scientist Galileo. He succeeded him as a professor of philosophy and mathematics at the Florentine Academy. Although Torricelli worked on many things, including the development of the microscope and telescope, he is best remembered for discovering the principle of the barometer. This came from working on something entirely different – the problem of draining water from flooded mines. "Lift pumps" were used for this work. But no one, not even Galileo, could explain why no lift pump would ever raise the water more than about 30 feet (10 meters).

Torricelli decided to try to find out why this happened. Instead of using a 30-foot column of water, he used mercury, which was much denser and so took up less space. From his findings, he was able to work out that air pressure determined how high the lift pump could raise water. He also noticed that the height of the column varied from day to day as the air pressure changed according to weather conditions.

Although Torricelli died before completing his work, others used his ideas to produce the instrument we now call the barometer. And because changes in air pressure usually take place before weather conditions change, the barometer is now one of the most important instruments used to forecast the weather.

Dr. Jonas Salk discovered a vaccine that prevented polio, a disease that often left people crippled for life. Polio was especially dangerous to children.

SPORT AND ENTERTAINMENT

AARON, Henry (Hank) Louis
1934–
U.S. baseball player

Hank Aaron was born in Mobile, Alabama. As a boy, he loved to play baseball, and as a teenager, he played for a time on a Negro League team in Indianapolis, Indiana. Then, in 1954, he started playing as an outfielder for the Milwaukee Braves, a team that later moved to Atlanta, Georgia, and became the Atlanta Braves.

Not only was Hank Aaron a good outfielder, but he was also an excellent hitter. He had a lifetime batting average of .305. As a major-league professional baseball player for 23 years, he hit the most career home runs (755), breaking Babe Ruth's record of 714. Aaron also holds the major-league career record for runs batted in (2,297). Twice, in 1955 and 1959, he won the National League's batting title. In 1957, he was named the National League's Most Valuable Player.

From 1954 through 1974, Hank Aaron played for the Milwaukee and then the Atlanta Braves in the National League. After playing two more seasons with the Milwaukee Brewers in the American League, Aaron retired. In 1982, he was elected to the Baseball Hall of Fame.

Hank Aaron had a lifetime batting average of .305.

ABDUL-JABBAR, Kareem
1947-
U.S. basketball player

Abdul-Jabbar ranks among the top basketball players in history. At 7 feet 2 inches (2.2 meters) tall, he had a height advantage in addition to quick, graceful movements and fine shooting. He was born Ferdinand Lewis (Lew) Alcindor, Jr., in New York City. He changed his name to Kareem Abdul-Jabbar when he adopted the Muslim religion in 1968.

Standing at 7 feet 2 inches tall, Kareem Abdul-Jabbar has scored 38,387 points in his career.

Photograph © 1988 Andrew D. Bernstein

At Power Memorial High School, he built a national reputation as a basketball center. After high school, he led the University of California at Los Angeles (UCLA) men's basketball team to National Collegiate Athletic Association (NCAA) championships in 1967, 1968, and 1969. During his years on the team, UCLA won 88 of its 90 games.

Following college graduation, he joined the Milwaukee Bucks of the National Basketball Association (NBA) and was voted Rookie of the Year. In 1975, he was traded to the Los Angeles Lakers, for whom he played until his retirement after the 1989 season.

Kareem Abdul-Jabbar is the NBA's all time leading scorer with 38,387 points. He played on six NBA championship teams and was the league's Most Valuable Player a record six times.

ALI, Muhammad (Cassius Clay)
1942-
U.S. boxer

When Cassius Clay was 12 years old he went to a policeman to report the loss of his bicycle. The policeman was supervising a boxing bout and invited the boy to join him. From that moment on, Clay was determined to become the greatest boxer in the world.

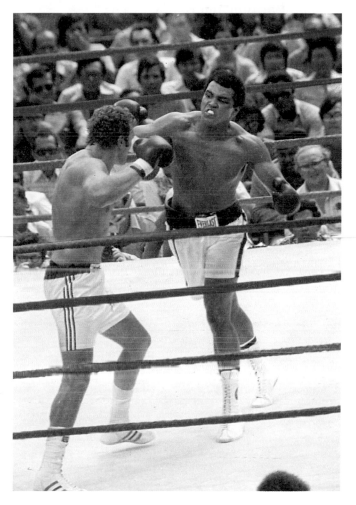

Muhammad Ali was the first person ever to win the world heavyweight title three times.

In 1960, at the end of his amateur career, Clay won a gold medal at the Olympic Games. In 1964, he took the professional world heavyweight title from Sonny Liston. His movements were lighter and faster than any other heavyweight boxer of the time. He said that he could "float like a butterfly, sting like a bee!" Soon after this bout Clay joined the Black Muslims, and changed his name to Muhammad Ali. His religious beliefs meant that he had to refuse army service. As a result the boxing authorities took away his world title in 1967.

Ali won back his title from George Foreman in 1974. In 1978 he lost it to Leon Spinks, but seven months later won it back again. Ali was the only man to win the world heavyweight title as many times. Soon afterwards he retired from boxing but came out of retirement several times, losing his final bout to Larry Holmes in 1980.

ARMSTRONG, (Daniel) Louis
1900–71
U.S. jazz musician

Armstrong was brought up in a children's home, where he learned to play cornet and trumpet. At this time, jazz was the most popular music in New Orleans (Armstrong's hometown), and after a few years he began playing with bands. In 1925, he formed his own bands, the Hot Five, the Hot Seven, and the Savoy Ballroom Five, to make records. These records helped to spread the sound of jazz around the world.

Armstrong played with great style and used higher notes than most trumpeters were willing to risk. He also sang, in a gruff, gravelly voice. He invented "scat" singing: putting nonsense syllables ("ba doo ba doo ba") to the notes of a jazz solo, "playing" his voice like an instrument. In 1947, he formed a band called the All Stars and he also played with other jazz musicians and bands. He had a warm-hearted personality and made many successful appearances in movies and on the Broadway stage as well as at jazz festivals. He was nicknamed "Satchmo." In 1964, his recording of "Hello Dolly" knocked even The Beatles from first place in the pop-music charts.

The jazz records of Louis Armstrong helped to spread the sound of jazz around the world.

BANNISTER, Roger
1929–
English athlete and doctor

Bannister trained to be a doctor at Oxford University. But he was also a talented athlete. On May 6, 1954, he became the first person ever to run the mile in less than four minutes. His world-record time was three minutes 59.4 seconds. Later the same year he won the 1500-meter race at the European Championships. In 1955, Bannister retired to take up his medical career.

English runner Roger Bannister was the first person ever to run the mile in less than four minutes.

BARNUM, Phineas Taylor (P.T.)
1810–91
U.S. showman

Barnum loved to organize exhibitions, shows, and theater performances. Wherever he could find an audience, he put on a show. And if no hall or theater was available, he set up a tent. He began his career in fairgrounds, showing off the famous dwarf "General Tom Thumb," talking dogs, and "mermaids." He became known throughout America in 1850 when he organized a tour for the popular Swedish opera singer Jenny Lind, who was known as the "Swedish Nightingale."

Barnum's worldwide fame began in 1871 when he started a touring circus modestly advertised as "The Greatest Show on Earth." In 1881, the show merged with James Bailey's circus, becoming the famous "Barnum and Bailey Circus."

A poster advertising Barnum and Bailey's circus.

BEATLES, The
1960–70
English pop music group

The Beatles were John Lennon (1940-80), Paul McCartney (born 1942), George Harrison (born 1943) and Ringo Starr (born Richard Starkey, 1940). The group began in 1956 as The Quarrymen in Liverpool, England. The group changed its name to The Silver Beatles in 1959 and to The Beatles in 1960. Pete Best was the original drummer but was later replaced by Ringo Starr. Their first hit was *Love Me Do* in 1962.

Helped by the publicity genius of manager Brian

The Beatles were a group of four musicians from Liverpool who became the world's best-known pop group.

Epstein and the skills of musical arranger George Martin, The Beatles quickly became the world's best-known pop group – and many people still regard them as the finest band in the whole history of pop. Lennon and McCartney wrote most of The Beatles's songs together. Harrison also wrote songs, often using ideas from Indian music. Starr played the drums and occasionally sang. For six years, the Beatles had hit after hit. Twenty-eight of their songs went into the Top Twenty on the record charts; seventeen reached number one. These included *She Loves You, I Want to Hold Your Hand, A Hard Day's Night, Paperback Writer,* and *Hey Jude.* In 1964 and 1965 they made two very successful comedy films, *A Hard Day's Night* and *Help!* In 1968 they provided voices and music for a fantasy cartoon film, *Yellow Submarine.*

People imitated their clothes, their hairstyles, their wisecracking humor, and above all their music. Almost all later pop bands learned from them. The strong feeling fans felt for them was known as "Beatlemania."

The band broke up in 1970.

BIRD, Larry
1956–
U.S. basketball player

A forward for the Boston Celtics of the National Basketball Association (NBA), Larry Bird has been called one of the best all-around players in the history of basketball. He is renowned for his shooting, passing, and rebounding.

Born in French Lick, Indiana, Bird attended Indiana State University from 1975 to 1979 and was a star player on their basketball team. He joined the Boston Celtics after graduation and was

Larry Bird has been called one of the best all-around players in the history of basketball.

named Rookie of the Year in his first season. With his help, the Celtics won three NBA championships: 1981, 1984, and 1986. Bird was named the NBA's Most Valuable Player three times: 1984, 1985, and 1986.

CHAMBERLAIN, Wilton Norman
1936–
U.S. basketball player

Nicknamed "Wilt the Stilt" because of his height (7 feet, 2 inches; or 2.2 meters), Chamberlain scored a record number of points for his college team, the University of Kansas. He left college to play professional basketball for the Harlem Globetrotters. From 1959 until 1973 he played in the National Basketball Association for the Philadelphia and San Francisco Warriors, the Philadelphia 76ers, and the Los Angeles Lakers. From 1959–65 he scored the most points in every season, including a (still unbroken) record of 100 points in a single game. He also holds the career record for the most rebounds and is second in career scoring to Kareem Abdul-Jabbar. He was elected to the Basketball Hall of Fame in 1978.

CHAPLIN, Sir Charles
1889–1977
English comedian and filmmaker

Charlie Chaplin had a hard childhood. His family lived in the London slums, and there was little money even for essentials like food and clothes. By the age of 8, Chaplin began performing on the music-hall stage, and before he was 18 he was a leading comedian.

Chaplin went to the United States in 1910, and almost at once began writing, directing, and performing in silent comedy films. He played the same character in most of them – a tramp with a bowler hat, a tiny moustache, pants far too big for him, a bamboo cane, and feet facing outward so that he waddled like a duck.

By the time Chaplin was 35, he was world famous. He specialized in slapstick: chases, fights, falls, and comic acrobatics. In *The Rink*, for example, the tramp saves a pretty girl from marrying a rich bully and is chased all over a roller-skating rink.

Once his fame was secure, Chaplin put serious ideas as well as funny ones into his films. In *The Kid*, for example, the tramp tries to save a 4-year-

Charlie Chaplin was famous for his costume, which consisted of a bowler hat, baggy trousers, a tight jacket and huge shoes.

old orphan from being put in a children's home. Among his many famous films are *Modern Times, The Great Dictator*, and *The Gold Rush*.

Chaplin was proud of the political ideas in his films, which show great sympathy for the suffering of the poor and hatred for the cruelty of war. These ideas were unusual in comedy films of the time and caused Chaplin trouble with the government, which branded him a communist. He moved his family to Switzerland, where he spent the rest of his life. He was given a special honorary Academy Award in 1972 and received a knighthood from Queen Elizabeth the Second of England in 1975.

CLEMENTE, Roberto
1934–72
Puerto Rican baseball player

A national hero in Puerto Rico, Roberto Clemente was one of the best baseball players of all time. He played as a right fielder for the Pittsburgh Pirates,

helping them to win the World Series in 1960 and 1971.

Known for his throwing, hitting, and fielding, Clemente was one of very few players in major-league history to get 3,000 hits. His career batting average was .317. He died in an airplane crash off the coast of Puerto Rico while trying to bring food and medicine to earthquake victims in Nicaragua.

Roberto Clemente, one of the few players in major-league history to get 3,000 hits.

COBB, Tyrus (Ty) Raymond
1886–1961
U.S. baseball player

Nicknamed "the Georgia Peach," Ty Cobb was one of the greatest players in the history of major-league baseball. Born in Narrows, Georgia, he began playing baseball as a child and was a professional player before he was 20. In 1905, the Detroit Tigers signed him to a contract.

Cobb still holds the record as the all-time leading hitter in the major leagues, with a .367 lifetime batting average. His career total of 4,191 hits was the major-league record until 1985, when it was broken by Pete Rose.

Cobb won 12 American League batting titles and was an expert base runner and base stealer. He

Ty Cobb was among the first five players to be elected to the Baseball Hall of Fame.

played mostly for the Detroit Tigers, serving as their player-manager from 1921 to 1926. He then played for the Philadelphia Athletics for two years before retiring. Getting more votes than anyone else, Ty Cobb was among the first five players elected to the Baseball Hall of Fame in 1936.

COSBY, William (Bill) Henry, Jr.
1937–
U.S. entertainer

Bill Cosby has excelled in many areas of the entertainment world. Mostly known as a comedian, he has also been very successful as a writer, movie actor, television star, creator of a children's cartoon series, advertising spokesperson for major companies, director, and producer.

Cosby was born into a poor family in Philadelphia, Pennsylvania. He drew many humorous ideas from life with his parents and two brothers. Today, many of his ideas come from family life with his wife, four daughters, and one son.

In many areas, Cosby broke new ground for blacks in show business. He was the first black to star in a television drama series, *I Spy*, which ran from 1965 to 1968. He won three Emmy awards for it.

Bill Cosby was the first black actor to star in a television drama series.

Bill Cosby's books and comedy albums have been very successful. And beginning in 1984, he starred in *The Cosby Show*, about a middle-class black family similar to his own; it ranks among the most popular comedies in television history.

DiMAGGIO, Joseph (Joe) Paul
1914–
U.S. baseball player

DiMaggio played for the New York Yankees for 13 seasons, between 1936-42 and 1946-51. From 1943-45 he fought in World War Two. DiMaggio was one of the best center fielders and hitters in the history of baseball. He had a lifetime batting average of .325 and hit a total of 361 home runs. He was voted Most Valuable Player in 1939, 1941, and 1947, and was elected to the Baseball Hall of Fame in 1955.

EVERT, Christine (Chris) Marie
1954–
U.S. tennis player

Chris Evert had already been playing tennis for ten years when, at 16, she was part of the winning U.S.A. team in the Wightman Cup matches. She went on to become one of the most technically skilled tennis players of the 1970s and 1980s. She was known for her accurate shots, her two-handed backhand, and her calm, steady concentration. She won many major tennis championships, including the U.S. Open, the French Open, and Wimbledon. Until her retirement in 1989, she worked to get her fellow women professionals prize money equal with men.

Chris Evert's calm, steady concentration helped her to win many major tennis championships. By the time she retired from professional tennis, she had become one of the most popular players on the circuit, not just with spectators but with her fellow players, including her arch rival, Martina Navratilova.

GEHRIG, Henry Louis (Lou)
1903–41
U.S. baseball player

Lou Gehrig was born in New York City. He attended Columbia University and played on the baseball team there. He was noticed by the New York Yankees, who signed him in 1923 to play for one of their farm teams. By 1925, he was playing first base for the Yankees in the major leagues. Gehrig was a great hitter. He had a lifetime batting average of .340 and hit 40 or more home runs in each of five seasons. Seven times, he had at least 150 runs batted in during a season. Because he played in 2,130 straight games without missing one, Gehrig was called the "Iron Horse."

Lou Gehrig played for the New York Yankees until 1939, when a disease called amyotrophic lateral sclerosis forced him to retire. No cure has ever been found for this muscle-weakening disease, which led to Gehrig's death in 1941. He was elected to the Baseball Hall of Fame in 1939.

Lou Gehrig played in 2,130 straight games without missing one.

GRETZKY, Wayne
1961–
Canadian ice hockey player

Each winter, Wayne Gretzky's father flooded the back yard of his home, and from the age of 3, Wayne skated on the family "ice rink." At 16, he was the youngest player and the top scorer of the Canadian team at the junior Ice Hockey World Cup. He turned professional in 1978, and he eventually joined the Edmonton Oilers of the National Hockey League. In the 1981-82 season, Gretzky set NHL records for number of goals (92), assists (120), and total points (212). In the 1985-86 season, he broke his own records, making 163 assists and scoring 215 total points. He was named

Canadian ice hockey player Wayne Gretzky was named Most Valuable Player in the NHL nine times.

Most Valuable Player in the NHL nine times. In 1988, he was traded to the Los Angeles Kings. A year later, he broke the NHL record for total career points (1,851).

HOUDINI, Harry
1874–1926
U.S. magician

"Harry Houdini" was the stage name of Ehrich Weiss. At first he was a trapeze artist, then a magician, and finally he began to specialize in daring escapes. His assistants would handcuff him, chain him, and lock him in a box and hang him high in the air or sink him underwater. Houdini would escape in seconds. To this day, no one knows how some of his tricks were done.

JACKSON, Michael
1958–
U.S. singer and dancer

When Jackson was 10 he toured the world with The Jackson Five (later known as The Jacksons), a group formed with his brothers. They stayed together for 14 years and had 25 hits. Jackson also began a solo career and had a hit with *Got to be There* when he was 14. His biggest hits are *Billie Jean* and the albums *Bad* and *Thriller* – two of the best selling LPs and music videos ever made.

Jackson is a unique singer, but a large part of the excitement of his performances is his dancing. He surrounds himself with highly trained dancers and uses wildly unusual routines and fantasy stories to accompany the music. The music video *Thriller*, for example, takes place in a graveyard and borrows ideas from old horror movies. Some critics consider Jackson the finest song-and-dance man of his time, a 1980s version of Fred Astaire.

Earvin Johnson, famous for his "no-look" pass and superior ball handling.

Michael Jackson's albums *Bad* and *Thriller* are two of the best selling LPs and music videos ever made.

JOHNSON, Earvin ("Magic")
1959–
U.S. basketball player

It seems that Earvin "Magic" Johnson can score whenever he wants to. His passing and ball-handling skills, including the "no-look" pass, make him a superior player as well. Born in Lansing, Michigan, Johnson started playing basketball in sixth grade. At home, he practiced by tossing rolled-up socks at imaginary baskets.

The three-time Michigan All-Stater earned the nickname "Magic" while in high school. As a sophomore at Michigan State University, Johnson, a 6-foot 9-inch guard, led his team to the National Collegiate Athletic Association (NCAA) championship. In 1981, after only two years in college, he signed with the Los Angeles Lakers in the National Basketball Association (NBA). Between 1982 and 1989, his team was in the NBA finals every year except 1986. The Lakers won the championship in 1982, 1985, 1987, and 1988. The first rookie to be voted Most Valuable Player in the

NBA championship finals (1982), Johnson was selected as the league's Most Valuable Player in 1987, 1989, and 1990.

JORDAN, Michael
1963–
U.S. basketball player

Jordan grew up in Wilmington, North Carolina. In high school he played all sports, but settled on basketball when he grew to 6 feet, 6 inches (2 meters) by his senior year. He attended the University of North Carolina on a basketball scholarship. He played so well that he was chosen for the All-American team in 1983. In 1984 he was a captain of the Summer Olympic basketball team that won the gold medal for the United States.

After his junior year in college, Jordan joined the Chicago Bulls professional basketball team. In his first season with the Bulls (1984-85) he led the league in scoring points and was named the National Basketball League's Rookie of the Year. He went on to lead the league in scoring in 1987, 1988, and 1989 and was named the league's Most Valuable Player in 1988.

Jordan is known for his ability to leap high into the air. At the height of his jump, he seems to "hang" there longer than is humanly possible before gravity pulls him back to the ground.

LOMBARDI, Vincent Thomas
1913–70
U.S. football coach

Vince Lombardi was born in Brooklyn, New York, and played football for Fordham University. When he was graduated, he took a job as a high-school football coach in New Jersey. In 1947 and 1948, he coached football at Fordham. From 1949 to 1953, he was a football coach at the U.S. Military Academy in West Point, New York. In 1954, Lombardi's career in professional football began when he became the offensive coach for the New York Giants. He became head coach of the Green Bay Packers in 1959 and was responsible for coaching them to five National Football League titles and to Super Bowl wins in 1967 and 1968. Because these were the first and second Super Bowls ever played, he was called "super coach." Vince Lombardi was known as a very strict coach who urged his players to perform to the best of their abilities. He coached the Washington Redskins for one season, in 1969, and then retired because of illness. He was elected to the Pro Football Hall of Fame in 1971, a year after his death.

Joe Louis was known as the "Brown bomber."

LOUIS, Joe
1914–81
U.S. boxer

Louis was a world heavyweight champion boxer for 12 years (1937-49). Born in Alabama, he grew up in Detroit, Michigan, where he learned to box. He was called the "Brown bomber." Louis successfully defended his heavyweight title 25 times. In his whole career he fought 71 professional fights and lost only three of them. He was elected to the Boxing Hall of Fame in 1954.

MAYS, Willie Howard
1931–
U.S. baseball player

From the time he was a little boy in Alabama, Mays practiced baseball. Because his high school had no baseball team, he played center field for the Birmingham Black Barons on weekends and during summer vacations. He was signed by the New York (later San Francisco) Giants in June 1950. Mays played for their minor league teams and was then moved up to the major leagues in May 1951.

Mays was the National League's Rookie of the Year in 1951. He was named its Most Valuable Player in 1954 and 1965. His career statistics are impressive – third in number of home runs (660), fourth in number of runs (2,062), and fifth in number of games played (2,992), among others. In 1972, Mays was traded to the New York Mets. He played with them for one season before his retirement. He was elected to the Baseball Hall of Fame in 1979, the first year he was eligible.

MONTANA, Joe
1956–
U.S. football player

As quarterback for the San Francisco 49ers in the National Football League, Joe Montana has been called one of the best in the history of the game. His leadership and skill on the field took his team to four Super Bowl victories between 1982 and 1990.

Born in Monongahela, Pennsylvania, Montana was an all-around star athlete in high school. He attended Notre Dame University on a football scholarship. There, he became known as the "Comeback Kid," for the many times he turned a

Joe Montana has been called one of the best players in the history of football.

losing game into a winning one during the last minutes. He was drafted by the San Francisco 49ers in 1979 and soon afterward became their starting quarterback.

Montana was named Most Valuable Player in the 1982, 1985, and 1990 Super Bowls. He holds many professional football records, among them leading lifetime completion percentage. His Super Bowl records include most touchdowns in one game – five.

OWENS, Jesse
1913-80
U.S. athlete

Owens came from a poor family. His grandparents had been slaves. His school coached him in sprinting and the long jump, and he was so talented that 28 universities offered him athletic scholarships. In 1935, while he was still a college student, he broke three world records and tied a fourth in forty-five minutes. In the 1936 Olympic Games Owens won gold medals in no fewer than four events, 100 meter and 200 meter races, the long jump, and the 400 meter relay. He set world records in the 200 meter race and the long jump and equaled the world record in the 100 meter race. After the Games, Owens turned professional, running against greyhounds and horses. Later, he was a supporter of Martin Luther King, Jr. His granddaughter carried the Olympic flame into the Los Angeles stadium for the Summer Games in 1984.

PELÉ (Edson Arantes do Nascimento)
1940–
Brazilian soccer player

Pelé was skilled in every aspect of soccer playing. He could control the ball equally well with his feet, head, or body. He began playing inside left forward for his country at the age of 16. In all, he made 111 appearances in international games, a world record. He was the most gifted member of a brilliant national team. During his career Brazil was considered one of the toughest teams to beat and one of the best to watch. Pelé scored more goals in his career than any other player: 1,281. He retired in 1971, but joined the New York Cosmos of the North American Soccer League in 1975. He played with them until 1977. His skill and famous name helped make professional soccer popular in the United States. Later, he began appearing in films and teaching children to play soccer. In 1985 he was given the title "Athlete of the Century."

As a young man, Jesse Owens showed so much talent that 28 universities offered him athletic scholarships.

Pele's skill and fame helped make professional soccer popular in the United States.

Elvis Presley was one of the first pop stars. His presence on stage was almost known to cause riots.

PRESLEY, Elvis Aaron

1935–77
U.S. singer and film star

Presley made his first record for his mother's birthday in 1953. A record company heard it and signed him up. His first hit, in 1956, was *Heartbreak Hotel*, and in the following year he made *All Shook Up*. More than any other performer, he made rock and roll music popular.

Presley was an unforgettable stage performer. He wore dazzling white suits with jewel studded lapels. He began making movies in the late 1950s. These include *Jailhouse Rock*, *GI Blues*, and *Blue Hawaii*. He went on singing and performing throughout the 1960s, and no fewer than 56 of his singles were hits. Some of his later songs had themes and melodies that made them popular with adults as well as younger listeners.

Presley's life ended tragically. After 1973, his health collapsed. In 1977, he died of a heart attack. His beautiful home, Graceland, is now a museum.

ROBINSON, Jack (Jackie) Roosevelt

1919–72
U.S. baseball player

Jackie Robinson was born in Cairo, Georgia. He starred in baseball, football, basketball, and track at the University of California at Los Angeles (UCLA). After college and service in the army as an officer in World War Two, he played baseball for the Kansas City Monarchs in the Negro League.

Robinson was so good that he was noticed by scouts for the major leagues. The Brooklyn Dodgers of the National League signed Robinson to a contract. In 1947, he became the first black to play for a major-league team. During that first season, he faced a great deal of racial prejudice. But Robinson persevered, finishing with a .297 batting average and Rookie of the Year honors.

During his professional baseball career with the Dodgers (1947-56), Jackie Robinson usually played second base. But he was also very good at the other infield positions and in the outfield. In 1949, he hit a league-leading .342 and was selected as the National League's Most Valuable Player. His lifetime batting average was .311. Because of his outstanding career, Robinson was elected to the Baseball Hall of Fame in 1962.

As a university student, Jackie Robinson starred in football, basketball and track, as well as baseball.

RUSSELL, William (Bill) Felton

1934–
U.S. basketball player and coach

Bill Russell grew up in Louisiana and later in Oakland, California, where he played high school basketball. Accepting an athletic scholarship to the University of San Francisco (1952-56), he led their basketball team to a record number of wins.

After graduation, he played on the 1956 gold-medal U.S. Olympic basketball team. He played professionally for the Boston Celtics from 1956 until 1969. From 1966, he was also the team's coach. During this time the team won 11 National Basketball Association (NBA) titles, and Russell was named the league's Most Valuable Player five times: in 1958, 1961, 1962, 1963, and 1965. He was second only to Wilt Chamberlain in career rebounds (21,620).

Russell retired briefly from basketball to become a television sportscaster, but he returned to coach the Seattle SuperSonics and other teams. Russell was elected to the Basketball Hall of Fame in 1975. He told his life story in *Go Up for Glory* (1966) and *Second Wind* (1979).

RUTH, Babe (George Herman)
1895–1948
U.S. baseball player

"Babe" Ruth was not only gifted as a pitcher and an outfielder, but he was a magnificent hitter. His frequent home runs (his record was 60 in one season,

Babe Ruth made the game of baseball more exciting and changed people's ideas about how baseball should be played.

in 1927) changed people's ideas about how baseball should be played. He made the game more exciting and attracted huge crowds. Babe Ruth played for the Boston Red Sox for six seasons and then the New York Yankees for 15 seasons. He set many records, including home runs in the American League for 12 seasons. He hit 714 home runs during his major league career, a record that was not broken until Henry Aaron passed it in 1974. He was elected to the Baseball Hall of Fame in 1936. He was known by many names, among them "the Sultan of Swat" and "the Bambino." Yankee Stadium became "the house that Ruth built."

THORPE, James Francis
1887-1953
U.S. athlete

Jim Thorpe was born on an Indian reservation in Oklahoma. As a young boy he participated in many sports and attended Haskell Institute in Lawrence, Kansas. Then he went to the Carlisle Indian School in Carlisle, Pennsylvania. Here, he did well in all sports, especially football. He was named to the All-American football team for two years (1911 and 1912). At Carlisle he also began training for the track and field events in the 1912 Olympic Games.

At the Stockholm (Sweden) Olympics, Thorpe won the pentathlon (a combination of five track and field events) and the decathlon (a combination of ten track and field events). This was the first time that one person had won both events. However, in 1913, it was discovered that Thorpe had played semiprofessional baseball in the summer of 1909. Because the Olympic Games were only for amateur athletes, his medals and records were taken away. In 1982 the Olympic Committee restored his records, and his medals were given to his family.

Thorpe played professional baseball from 1913 to 1919. He helped to establish the American Professional Football Association (later the National Football League) and served as its president. He played for various football teams from 1915 to 1929.

He returned to Oklahoma in 1937 and became involved in Indian affairs. In 1950, Jim Thorpe was voted the greatest male athlete and greatest football player of the first half of the twentieth century. His life was recounted in the motion picture, *Jim Thorpe, All-American* (1951).

WILLIAMS, Theodore (Ted) Samuel
1918–
U.S. baseball player

Ted Williams was born in San Diego, California, and became one of the greatest baseball hitters of all time. He began his career in 1939 when he was signed to play in the outfield for the Boston Red Sox of the American League. He went on to play for the Red Sox until 1960, missing five seasons while serving in World War Two and the Korean War as a bomber pilot.

For the Red Sox, Williams had a career batting average of .344. He batted .406 in 1941, the last time any major leaguer hit over .400. In 1942 and 1947, Ted Williams won the American League Triple Crown, leading in home runs, batting average, and runs batted in. Twice, in 1946 and in 1949, he was named the American League's Most Valuable Player. The last at-bat of his 19-year career came at the end of the 1960 season – and he hit a home run! He finished with 521 lifetime home runs. Ted Williams was elected to the Baseball Hall of Fame in 1966.

Babe Zaharias was a versatile athlete who achieved Olympic and professional success.

Ted Williams was named the American League's Most Valuable Player twice and was elected to the Baseball Hall of Fame in 1966.

ZAHARIAS, Mildred (Babe) Didrikson
1914–56
U.S. athlete

Babe Didrikson Zaharias was one of the most talented athletes of all time. When she was 16 years old, she broke the world javelin record. Zaharias also excelled at basketball and baseball.

At the 1932 Olympics, Zaharias set world records and won gold medals in the javelin and 80-meter hurdles. She also won a silver medal in the high jump. She is the only person ever to have won Olympic medals in running, jumping, and throwing.

Throughout her life, Babe Zaharias showed talent at every sport, from boxing and fencing to billiards and tennis. After the 1932 Olympics, she turned professional, giving athletic exhibitions. She then learned golf. In 1946 and 1947, she won 17 golf tournaments in a row. In 1950, an Associated Press poll named her the most outstanding woman athlete of the first half of the twentieth century.

Born in Port Arthur, Texas, Babe Didrikson Zaharias played baseball even as a child. Because of the home runs she used to hit then, she was nicknamed "Babe" after Babe Ruth.

THINKERS AND INVENTORS

ARISTOTLE
384–322 BC
Greek thinker

When Aristotle was 17, he went to study with Plato in Athens and stayed there until he was nearly 40. After some years as a traveling professor (one of his pupils was the young Prince Alexander of Macedon, later Alexander the Great), he returned to Athens in 334 BC, to set up the school known as the Lyceum.

From boyhood, Aristotle studied everything in nature, displaying a wide range of interests. He wrote on many different subjects such as plants,

Aristotle is considered the most important thinker of ancient Greece.

marine creatures, and the diseases of bees. He organized all Earth's creatures into categories, progressing from the simplest (plants) to the most complex (human beings). He studied the nature of the universe, and this led him to lecture and write about rocks, weather, and the "elements" (earth, air, fire, water, ether) from which he said everything was made. (Ether was the name given to the element that people of Aristotle's time thought filled space beyond the Earth's atmosphere.) He developed a way of studying similar to what we now call "scientific method." Going from one step to the next, he would consider each new fact in turn until a whole pattern of ideas was logically built up.

Later in his life, Aristotle used the same logical method to study humans and their activities. He was particularly interested in "ethics": the way we organize our daily lives and deal with other people. He wrote books on law, politics, religion, and human nature. His lectures became world-famous, and many rulers, statesmen, and aristocrats sent their sons to learn from him. His ideas were rediscovered during the Middle Ages and have had a great influence on later thinkers and scholars.

BELL, Alexander Graham
1847–1922
Scottish-born U.S. inventor

Bell came from a family of well-known speech therapists in Edinburgh, Scotland. He was trained to follow in his father's footsteps. He studied the way that ears receive sound and devised all kinds of hearing aids. The family moved to Canada in 1870, and two years later, Bell opened a school near Boston to teach speech to deaf people, using his father's system. One day, while testing microphones and receivers, one of his assistants, an electrical engineer, twanged a wire by mistake. The sound traveled down the wire so clearly that Bell could hear it in the next room. Bell wondered if speech could be sent down wires in the same way, and began experimenting. The result was the tele-

When he invented the telephone, Alexander Graham Bell was actually trying to find ways of helping deaf people hear again.

phone. Bell, then aged 29, patented the telephone in 1876. The Bell Telephone Company, which he founded in 1877, was the largest phone company in the world for many years.

Bell invented other things as well. He built kites big enough to carry people, a hydrofoil boat that set the world water speed record in 1918, and the photophone, an early machine for transmitting through light rays. He also invented a wax cylinder record for phonographs.

BESSEMER, Henry
1813–98
English inventor

When people imagine inventors as eccentric geniuses, Bessemer is the kind of person they have in mind. He spent all his life inventing and patented no fewer than 114 different gadgets and ideas. Two of his inventions are artificial gold dust (made from brass) for gold paint and the first type-setting machine used in printing. He is best remembered for the "Bessemer process," a way of turning pig iron (crude iron) into steel by removing impurities such as carbon.

The English engineer Henry Bessemer invented a method of producing large quantities of steel in 1856.

BRAILLE, Louis
1809–52
French teacher

Braille, who was blind himself, was a teacher at the National Institute for the Blind in Paris. He is remembered today for inventing the Braille alphabet. He adapted a system used in the French army called "night writing." This used 12 raised dots in various patterns that could be "written" and "read" in the dark by feeling them. Braille reduced the number of dots to six and worked out an alphabet to enable blind people to read with their fingertips.

CONFUCIUS (K'ung Fu-Tzu)
about 551–479 BC
Chinese thinker

Like many early thinkers, for example Buddha or Socrates, Confucius was interested in what "goodness" was, whether it could be taught and learned, and what sort of life a "good" person ought to lead. He traveled from town to town, studying and teaching, and when he was too old to travel he settled down and continued his teaching. He also edited classical texts and may have done some writing. The *Analects*, a collection of Confucius's conversations, lectures, and sayings, was put together by some of his pupils after his death.

By the time Confucius died, he was considered one of the greatest thinkers China had ever known.

Confucius was renowned for his many sayings. Two of the most famous are: "Never do to others what what you would not like them to do to you" and "People control principles; principles do not control people."

EASTMAN, George
1854–1932
U.S. inventor

Until Eastman's time, photographs were made using sheets of glass or copper. They were large, awkward to handle, and expensive. Eastman experimented by putting a layer of gelatin on a strip of paper. He found that this produced photos just as clearly and far more easily.

Eastman called his invention "film strip" or "film." It was cheap, and the cameras Eastman made for it were small and easy to carry. They were not like the heavy wooden cameras people had used before. Eastman's inventions made photography a popular hobby. In 1899, he improved film still further by using celluloid instead of paper as the film's base.

George Eastman's inventions made photography a popular hobby.

EDISON, Thomas Alva
1847–1931
U.S. inventor

Even as a child, Edison was fascinated by the way things worked. He spent only three months at school in his entire life. He worked as a newsboy and later as a clerk in the U.S. telegraph office, sending Morse code messages from town to town. Edison liked to take things apart to see how they worked. Soon after figuring out how the telegraph worked, he was patenting improvements on the equipment that made him a millionaire.

In 1876, Edison built a laboratory (he called it an "invention factory") in New Jersey to try out new ideas, and hired a staff of scientists. He would sketch out ideas and give them to his employees to make. In the years that followed, the Edison company patented over 1,000 new inventions, including the phonograph (ancestor of the record player), the film projector, the carbon microphone (the one inside a telephone), and the electric light bulb. Edison was one of the most successful inventors in history.

FRANKLIN, Benjamin
1706–90
U.S. statesman, printer, and inventor

Franklin hated delays and untidiness. If something needed to be done, he did it as quickly as possible. Every morning he wrote down in his diary one or two good qualities, for instance kindness and patience, and tried to live up to them all day. A printer by trade, he wrote and edited a newspaper called *Poor Richard's Almanack*. It contained poli-

Thomas Edison liked to take things apart and see how they worked and he ultimately became one of the most successful inventors in history. He is shown here with just one of his inventions, exhausted after hours of work.

Benjamin Franklin flew a kite in a thunderstorm in order to show that lightning is a form of electricity. It was a very dangerous thing to do. Others had been killed by lightning trying to do the same thing.

tical news and advice on how to live a healthy and happy life. Famous proverbs and wise remarks such as "those who hesitate are lost" and "early to bed and early to rise make a man healthy, wealthy, and wise" come from Franklin's newspaper.

In his spare time Franklin studied the works of thinkers and scientists of the past. In 1743, he founded the American Philosophical Society to discuss ideas. He was also an inventor, although he had no scientific training. When he found out that he could see perfectly well at a distance, but had blurred sight up close, he invented bifocal lenses for his glasses. In 1752, he invented the lightning rod. It was a device to attach to the roof of a building to attract electrical discharge from lightning. The electricity was then carried harmlessly into

the earth. His experiments also proved the existence of static (natural) electricity.

Above all, Franklin believed that "no man is an island," an idea he found in a poem by John Donne, an Englishman. He believed we all live in a community with other human beings, and we should try to understand and help them. This led him to action. Franklin became a town councilman, and organized mail deliveries, a fire fighting service, the first free public library, and the first street lighting in America. He spent 21 years as deputy postmaster general for the American Colonies while they were still under British rule.

In 1776, at the age of 70, Franklin decided to help the American Revolution and joined Thomas Jefferson and the other leaders who prepared the Declaration of Independence. During the war he served as an ambassador to France. He also helped to negotiate the peace treaty with Britain that ended the war. When Franklin was 81, he became a member of the Constitutional Convention that wrote the U.S. Constitution.

FULTON, Robert
1765–1815
U.S. inventor

Fulton designed the first successful steam-powered boat, which he demonstrated on the Seine River in France. He then returned to his native country, and in 1807 a steamboat he designed made the 150-mile (240-kilometer) trip up the Hudson River from New York City to Albany. This marked the beginning of a new way for ships to travel by water. In the next few years, Fulton designed 17 more steamboats.

Earlier, Fulton also built one of the first submarines. It held four people and used water tanks for ballast. These were filled to make the craft submerge and pumped empty to make it rise to the surface. The submarine was powered by hand; the passengers turned handles to crank the propeller-shaft. Fulton took his invention to France, hoping that the French government would use submarines in their war against the English. But the French thought it would not be fair to conduct underwater warfare, and Fulton went back to the United States. His plans remained in Paris, however, and 60 years later the writer Jules Verne read them. He used Fulton's idea of the submarine in his novel *Twenty Thousand Leagues under the Sea*. He even called his ship *Nautilus*, after Fulton's submarine.

Robert Fulton designed the first successful steam-powered boat which he demonstrated on the Seine River in France.

GODDARD, Robert Hutchings
1882–1945
U.S. inventor

Early rockets used gunpowder, a heavy and unstable fuel. It was fine in fireworks, but useless for larger rockets intended to lift objects or people into space. Goddard invented a new kind of rocket, powered by liquid gas. He hoped that it might be used to launch space vehicles, but the government ignored his ideas. It was not until Werner von Braun and his fellow German scientists joined NASA after World War Two that Goddard's rockets were developed – and advanced versions of them are still used today. Goddard also devised a way of steering rockets in space by changing the direction of the engine jets. He invented the "multistage" rocket, which throws off each engine section as its job is done.

GUTENBERG, Johannes
1395?–1468?
German inventor

Before Gutenberg, there were no printed books. The Chinese inventor Pi Sheng had devised a method of printing in the eleventh century, but it was only used for playing cards. Every book had to be written by hand, so books were expensive and rare. Gutenberg realized that if each letter of the alphabet were carved on woodblocks, they could be used and reused to make words and lines of type. The wooden blocks provided the pattern or mold needed to cast the type in metal. Each letter was carved backward, so that when the metal type was inked and pressed onto paper, the words read correctly.

Gutenberg spent several years making blocks and letters small enough. In 1448 he was ready to print a full-length book using his movable type method. He went into business with Johann Fust, who provided money for a factory, but they quarrelled, and Gutenberg went out on his own. It took him seven years to produce 300 copies of the Bible, each containing 1,282 pages, as well as copies of a Latin grammar text – the first printed books.

The work of Johannes Gutenberg changed history. He invented the printing press, allowing books to be widely available to many people.

HOLLAND, John Philip
1841–1914
Irish-born U.S. inventor

For centuries, inventors had dreamed of the submarine, a boat which would travel underwater. The problem was not the air supply, but how the boat was to be moved. Early submarines were one-person glass bubbles, dragged along by ropes from the surface or rowed awkwardly through leather-protected holes which were seldom as waterproof as they were supposed to be. Holland invented a submarine powered by an engine. It used gasoline when it was on the surface and the exhaust gases could escape; underwater, it used electric power from enormous batteries.

John Philip Holland invented the first submarine powered by an engine.

McCORMICK, Cyrus Hall
1809–84
U.S. inventor

Born on a farm in Virginia, McCormick became a self-made millionaire. He did so by inventing the first practical reaper, a machine for harvesting grain. Until his invention, most harvesting had been done by hand. McCormick's machine could replace dozens of laborers and allow just a few workers to farm huge tracts of land. Today's huge combine-harvesters are modern versions of McCormick's original reaper.

Farming the land using McCormick's combine harvester.

MARCONI, Guglielmo
1874–1937
Italian inventor

In 1894 Marconi read a newspaper story about electromagnetic waves – electrical/magnetic energy moving through the air. They cannot be seen, heard, or felt. Marconi was very interested to read that the waves traveled through space at the speed of 186,000 miles (300,000 kilometers) per second. He wondered if they could be used to send messages.

To make electromagnetic waves carry messages, two things were needed: a way to change them and a way to receive the changed waves (in other words, a transmitter and a receiver). Marconi began experimenting in his attic. After months of trying, Marconi succeeded. In 1895 he found that he could send the interference (changed waves) all the way across the room, then down through the floors of the house to ring an electric bell. This happened in the middle of the night, and surprised the servants. The waves continued through the window to a receiving ring in the garden and finally went across fields and woods to a ring on the opposite side of a nearby hill. His brother fired a gun to show that the message had been received.

The Italian government was not interested in Marconi's work. So, a year later, he went to London and showed the officials of the British Post Office that "wireless" messages (messages sent without wires) could be sent as far as 1,000 feet (300 meters). The Post Office gave him money to continue his work. In the next few years he slowly increased the distance his messages could go: across the Bristol Channel from England to Wales, across the English Channel from England to France, and finally, in 1901, across the Atlantic Ocean from England to Newfoundland in Canada.

Marconi founded the Wireless Telegraph and Signal Company to perfect "wireless telegraphy." His work won him the Nobel Prize in physics in 1909. It led to today's worldwide radio communication systems.

MARX, Karl
1818–83
German thinker and writer

Of all nineteenth century thinkers, few have changed modern life as much as Marx. His theories have affected modern politics, philosophy (the study of basic beliefs), economics, and sociology (the study of how people get along with each other). He thought that the way most countries set up

Karl Marx discusses his theories with workers. His ideas, known as "Marxism," have influenced communist countries throughout the world.

their industry, trade, and farming was wrong, because it gave wealth to only a few people. He suggested a new system of equal shares and rights for all. His ideas, known as "Marxism," shaped the government and economies of almost all communist (or Marxist) countries in the world.

Marx said that in most countries, all through history, there have been two main groups of people. The first group, "capitalists," own farms and businesses. The second group, the "proletariat," work for capitalists.

Workers have nothing but their own power to work. No matter how hard they struggle, they still end up with nothing else. Capitalists, on the other hand, make profits (money left after paying business costs) and grow richer every year. Marx said that the only way to make a fairer system was by revolution (to overthrow, or get rid of, the government). The workers should take all businesses and property into their own hands and run a "workers' state" in which everyone is equal. For a time this state would be a "dictatorship of the proletariat" in which everyone has to forget their own interests and put the state first. But the state would "wither away," as Marx put it. Fairness and equality would

rule. There would be no need for a congress, government, civil police forces, or managers.

Marx was a quiet man, who was often sick. He never took an active part in revolutions, spoke at meetings, organized strikes, or went on demonstrations. He stayed at home to write. When his books caused riots and he was forced to leave one country after another, he showed no surprise. He settled at last in London, where he spent the last 34 years of his life. His friend Friedrich Engels gave him enough money to live and helped him with his books, especially *Das Kapital* and the *Communist Manifesto*, which set out his revolutionary ideas.

NOBEL, Alfred
1833–96
Swedish inventor

Before Nobel, explosives were awkward and dangerous to handle. Gunpowder was hard to measure out without spilling. Also, it was so full of impurities that it was dangerously unreliable. The other main explosive was nitroglycerine. This is a liquid so ready to explode that the slightest knock can set it off. Nobel mixed nitroglycerine with an inert material (one that would not explode). This made it safe to carry. He called the new explosive dynamite ("the powerful one"). Its development made him a multimillionaire.

Nobel always claimed that he had expected dynamite to be used only for peaceful purposes such as blasting rock in quarries. He was horrified when people began using it for war. So, when he died, he did not leave his fortune to his children. Instead, he left large sums to give prizes each year to men or women who had done most to benefit humanity. Nobel Prizes are given for discoveries in physics, chemistry, medicine, and literature. A prize also goes to the person who has worked hardest for peace throughout the year. (A sixth prize, for economics, was added after Nobel's death.)

As well as inventing dynamite, Nobel invented blasting jelly and smokeless gunpowder. When he died in 1896, he left over $9,000,000 to be used for prizes for human achievements.

PLATO
about 427–347 BC
Greek thinker

Plato was an Athenian nobleman and had considered a career in politics. But he disliked the arguments and lies of those in power. So, he went to study with Socrates, thought to be the most honest man in Athens. Plato became a teacher himself. In warm weather he would teach his students in a wood called Academia. Two words for centers of learning, "academy" and "academe," are derived from this name.

Plato believed that everything there is – from mice to tables, from memory to love – has a perfect form. What we see, feel, or know is a blurred version of that perfect form. It is changed from its perfect form by our other feelings and senses. By concentrating hard, by clearing our minds of unnecessary thoughts, we will gradually work out the simple truth about everything. He thought that human creations such as law and politics also had perfect forms. He believed that if we can discover them our lives will be transformed. He tried to turn Syracuse in Sicily into a perfect state with an ideal king, but the experiment failed because the king, Dionysius II, was ill. Plato's teaching brought him pupils from all over Greece.

Plato wrote dozens of books. They take the form of "dialogues" (conversations) and "epistles" (letters). One of the best-known is *The Republic*, in which he explains his views on the ideal state. Plato's teaching and his methods have been admired throughout the centuries. Many of his views are still taught today.

Socrates was the leading philosopher and teacher of his time in Greece. His ideas have influenced people throughout the ages.

Plato was a philosopher and writer. He was also a friend and pupil of another Greek thinker named Socrates.

SOCRATES
about 469-399 BC
Greek thinker

When Socrates was a young man he asked Apollo's oracle, "Who is the wisest person in the world?" (An oracle is a person believed by some ancient people to speak the truth as directly handed down by the gods.) The oracle answered, "Socrates." After asking everyone who seemed wise what they knew, Socrates decided that he was the wisest because he was the only one who knew how little he really knew. He developed a system of investigation by questioning. To find out about anything, question after question has to be asked. As wrong ideas are eliminated, the questioner ends with a clearer idea of the problem than at the start.

Socrates's main interest was human nature. He wanted to know why we behave as we do, and how we can be better. He believed that philosophy (the search for wisdom and the study of beliefs) should be applied to life. He therefore did not believe in ready-made rules for success offered by some philosophers. He believed that to be good we must know what "good" means. Socrates often asked such questions as "What is truth?" His questions were ridiculed by some people, including the Greek playwright Aristophanes. In his comedy *Clouds* Aristophanes made fun of Socrates as a kind of crazy professor who understood nothing about daily life. But others, especially young people, found his ideas exciting and flocked to learn from him. The government feared he would stir up trouble. Socrates was put on trial and condemned to death for denying the existence of the gods and for "corrupting the young." He had to drink a poison (hemlock), and, while it took effect, spent his last hours with his friends discussing whether the soul lives on after the body dies.

Socrates left no writings. His teaching survives mainly in the works of two of his followers, Plato and Xenophon. His ideas inspired many later thinkers, from Aristotle to Cicero to those of modern times. He was respected by Christians for his teaching about such matters as love.

Following the example of Henry David Thoreau, many people take vacations in the wilderness hoping to "discover themselves."

raise money for that war, he refused to pay it, and gladly went to jail for the night. Thoreau's most famous essay, *Civil Disobedience*, explained his views on government and the individual person.

In his 40s he often went on long journeys by himself, and later wrote about them. On one trip he caught a chill which developed into tuberculosis, and caused his death.

THOREAU, Henry David
1817–62
U.S. thinker and writer

When Thoreau left Harvard University, he worked as a teacher. His favorite ways to spend time were walking and canoeing. He liked to be alone with nature and his own thoughts. In 1841, he made friends with Ralph Waldo Emerson (1803-82) a famous writer.

In 1845 Thoreau went to live alone in a cabin in the woods beside Walden Pond in Concord, Massachusetts. He lived there for two years. He wrote a book, *Walden*, which described his thoughts during this time.

Walden was enormously popular, and many people today take vacations in the "wilderness," hoping to "discover themselves" as Thoreau did.

When Thoreau left Walden, he supported the American Indians' struggle against the U.S. government. He spoke out against slavery and the war being fought against Mexico. When the government imposed a poll tax (requiring people to pay money before they could vote in an election) to

WASHINGTON, Booker Taliaferro
1856–1915
U.S. educator

Washington, the son of slaves, grew up in Virginia. When slaves were freed by the government in 1865, he moved with his family to West Virginia. He worked and went to school at the same time. When he was 16 he entered Hampton Institute, a school for blacks, in Virginia. After graduation in 1875, he took courses in Washington, D.C., and then returned in 1879 to Hampton Institute to teach.

In 1881, Washington started Tuskegee Normal and Industrial Institute in Tuskegee, Alabama, for blacks. He believed that it was important for blacks to become economically independent. At Tuskegee Institute, as it became known, poor students could come and learn a trade or become teachers. Another teacher there was George Washington Carver.

Washington soon became a leader and spokesman for the black people. His opinions were respected by presidents Theodore Roosevelt and William Howard Taft and other members of the government. He raised money for black causes, and he contributed his own money too.

WATT, James
1736–1819
Scottish inventor

Although other people were experimenting with steam power in the first half of the eighteenth century, James Watt was the first person to make a cheap, efficient steam engine. His engine was used to drive machinery, and it soon replaced the water wheel as the main source of power in factories. Watt came up with the word *horsepower* to describe an engine's efficiency. A 20-horsepower engine, for example, is supposed to have the power of 20 horses.

In his spare time, Watt experimented with gases and electricity. The *watt*, a unit of measurement for electrical power, is named after him.

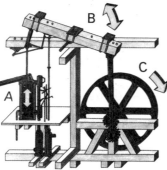

Here is a diagram of Watt's steam engine. Steam in the cylinder (A) moves the beam (B) which is connected to the flywheel (C). Belts or chains can then be attached to the flywheel to drive other machinery.

WHITNEY, Eli
1765–1825
U.S. inventor

Whitney invented the cotton gin, a machine for separating the fluffy fibers of the cotton flower from the seeds and other waste. The fibers could then be spun and woven into cloth. Each Whitney machine did the work of a dozen people and made it possible for thousands of farms in the southern United States to take up cotton production. But the idea behind the cotton gin was so simple that planters could steal it without paying Whitney anything for his invention. Desperate for money, Whitney started making guns. In 1798, the American government asked Whitney for 10,000 rifles for the army. He took eight years to complete a two-year contract. But he was the first to develop a new way to make the rifles. One group of people made all the wooden parts, another made the metal parts, and a third group assembled the finished guns. This way, the rifle parts were interchangeable. If one part wore out or was broken, it could be replaced. It was the beginning of manufacturing using mass production.

WRIGHT, Wilbur
1867–1912
U.S. air pioneer
and

WRIGHT, Orville
1871–1948
U.S. air pioneer

In the 1890s, the Wright brothers ran a bicycle shop. Their hobby was designing aircraft. They were determined to be the first people in the world to fly in a machine that was "heavier than air." They studied the reports of earlier pioneers, including Otto Lilienthal. Then they designed machines of their own, using bicycle tubes and pipes to build frames and covering them with cloth or paper to make the fuselage and wings.

In 1903 the brothers made the very first powered flight. It lasted for 12 seconds and covered over 120 feet (37 meters). Two years later they were able to stay airborne for over half an hour, and flew 24.2 miles (38.9 kilometers). They patented their flying machine in 1906, and toured the U.S.A. showing people that flying was safe and fun. In 1909, the U.S. Army began to use planes for reconnaissance (flying over land or sea to see what the enemy was doing). The Wrights formed an aircraft-manufacturing company in the same year.

The air pioneers, Orville and Wilbur Wright, are shown here with one of their early aircraft.

INDEX

Aaron, Henry (Hank) Louis 72
Abdul-Jabbar, Kareem 72
Addams, Jane 44
Aesop 7
Alcott, Louisa May 7
Alexander the Great (Alexandros) 25
Ali, Muhammad (Cassius Clay) 73
Andersen, Hans Christian 7
Anthony, Susan Brownell 44
Archimedes 60
Aristotle 85
Armstrong, (Daniel) Louis 73
Armstrong, Neil 44
Attila 25
Augustus (Gaius Julius Caesar Octavianus) 26

Bach, Johann Sebastian 8
Bannister, Roger 74
Banting, Frederick Grant 60
Barnum, Phineas Taylor (P.T.) 74
Barrie, James Matthew 8
Barton, Clara 45
Baum, L. (Lyman) Frank 8
Beatles, The 74
Beethoven, Ludwig van 9
Bell, Alexander Graham 85
Bessemer, Henry 86
Bird, Larry 75
Bismark, Otto Eduard Leopold von 26
Blériot, Louis 15
Bolívar, Simón 45
Boone, Daniel 46
Bowie, Jim 46
Boyle, Robert 60
Brahms, Johannes 9
Braille, Louis 86
Burbank, Luther 61
Burnett, Frances Hodgson 9
Byrd, Richard Evelyn 46

Cabot, John (Giovanni Caboto) 46
Cabot, Sebastian 46
Caesar, Gaius Julius 27
Carroll, Lewis 10
Carver, George Washington 61
Cassatt, Mary 10
Cavendish, Henry 61
Chamberlain, Wilton Norman 75
Champlain, Samuel de 47
Chaplin, Charles 75
Charlemagne 27
Chaucer, Geoffrey 10
Chopin, Frédéric 10
Churchill, Winston Leonard Spencer 28
Clark, William 55
Clemente, Roberto 76
Cleopatra 28
Cobb, Tyrus (Ty) Raymond 76
Cody, William Frederick (Buffalo Bill) 47
Columbus, Christopher 48

Confucius (K'ung Fu-Tzu) 86
Cook, James 48
Copernicus, Nicolaus 62
Cortés, Hernán (Hernando Cortez) 49
Cosby, William (Bill) Henry 77
Cousteau, Jacques-Yves 49
Crockett, Davy 50
Curie, Marie 62
Curie, Pierre 62
Custer, George Armstrong 50

Da Gama, Vasco 50
Darwin, Charles Robert 62
Da Vinci, Leonardo 11
Defoe, Daniel 11
Degas, Hilaire Germain Edgar 12
Dickens, Charles 12
DiMaggio, Joseph (Joe) Paul 77
Douglass, Frederick 51
Doyle, Arthur Conan 12
Drake, Francis 51

Earhart, Amelia 52
Eastman, George 87
Edison, Thomas Alva 87
Einstein, Albert 63
Elizabeth the First 29
Ericson, Leif 52
Evert, Christine (Chris) Marie 77

Fahrenheit, Gabriel Daniel 64
Faraday, Michael 64
Fermi, Enrico 64
Fleming, Alexander 65
Ford, Henry 52
Franklin, Benjamin 87
Fulton, Robert 88

Galileo 65
Gandhi, Mohandas Karamchand 30
Gauguin, Paul 13
Gehrig, Henry Louis (Lou) 78
Genghis Khan (Temujin) 30
Goddard, Robert Hutchings 89
Gorbachev, Mikhail Sergeevich 30
Grahame, Kenneth 13
Gretzky, Wayne 78
Grimm, Jakob Ludwig 13
Grimm, Wilhelm Karl 13
Gutenberg, Johannes 89

Henry the Eighth 31
Hickok, James Butler (Wild Bill) 53
Hippocrates (Hippokrates) 66
Hitler, Adolf 32
Holland, John Philip 90
Homer (Homeros) 14
Houdini, Harry 78
Hubble, Edwin 66
Hudson, Henry 53

Irving, Washington 14

Jackson, Andrew 32
Jackson, Michael 78
Jefferson, Thomas 33
Jenner, Edward 67
Johnson, Earvin ("Magic") 79
Jones, John Paul 53
Jordan, Michael 79
Joseph, Chief 33

Keller, Helen Adams 54
Kepler, Johannes 67
Khomeini, Ayatollah Ruhollah 34
King, Martin Luther, Jr. 54
Kipling, Rudyard 15
Kublai Khan 34

Lavoisier, Antoine Laurent 68
Leakey, Louis Seymour Bazett 68
Lee, Robert Edward 35
Leeuwenhoek, Anton van 68
Lenin, Vladimir Ilyich 35
Lewis, Meriwether 55
Lincoln, Abraham 36
Lindbergh, Charles Augustus 55
Linnaeus, Carolus (Carl von Linné) 68
Lombardi, Vincent Thomas 79
London, Jack 15
Louis the Fourteenth 37
Louis, Joe 80

McCormick, Cyrus Hall 90
Magellan, Ferdinand 56
Mandela, Nelson Rolihlahla 56
Mao Zedong (Mao Tse-tung) 37
Marconi, Guglielmo 90
Marx, Karl 90
Mays, Willie Howard 80
Melville, Herman 15
Michelangelo 16
Montana, Joe 80
Moses, Grandma (Anna Mary) 16
Mozart, Wolfgang Amadeus 17

Napoleon the First 38
Newton, Isaac 68
Nightingale, Florence 56
Nobel, Alfred 91

O'Keeffe, Georgia 17
Owens, Jesse 81

Pasteur, Louis 70
Peary, Robert Edwin 57
Pelé (Edson Arantes do Nascimento) 81
Penn, William 57
Perrault, Charles 18

Peter the First ("the Great") 39
Picasso, Pablo Ruiz y 18
Pizarro, Francisco 57
Plato 92
Poe, Edgar Allan 19
Polo, Marco 58
Potter, Helen Beatrix 19
Presley, Elvis Aaron 82
Priestley, Joseph 70

Raleigh, Walter 58
Rembrandt (Rembrandt Harmenszoon van Rijn) 19
Revere, Paul 58
Robinson, Jack (Jackie) Roosevelt 82
Roosevelt, Franklin Delano 39
Roosevelt, Theodore 40
Russell, Bill (William Felton Russell) 82
Ruth, Babe (George Herman) 83

Sacajawea 59
Salk, Jonas Edward 71
Sendak, Maurice 20
Sewell, Anna 20
Shakespeare, William 21
Sitting Bull, Chief 41
Socrates (Sokrates) 92
Stalin, Joseph 41
Steinbeck, John 22
Stevenson, Robert Louis 22
Sullivan, Anne 59
Sun Yat-sen 42
Swift, Jonathan 22

Tchaikovsky, Peter Ilich 23
Tecumseh 42
Thatcher, Margaret 42
Thoreau, Henry David 93
Thorpe, James Francis 83
Tolkien, J.R.R. 23
Torricelli, Evangelista 71
Tubman, Harriet 59
Twain, Mark (Samuel Clemens) 23

Van Gogh, Vincent 24
Verne, Jules 24

Washington, Booker Taliaferro 93
Washington, George 43
Watt, James 94
Whitney, Eli 94
Wilder, Laura Ingalls 24
Williams, Theodore (Ted) Samuel 84
Wright, Orville 94
Wright, Wilbur 94

Zaharias, Mildred (Babe) Didrikson 84